# SMILERS

## PART THREE: SKILLS FOR ENTERPRISE

# SMILERS

## PART THREE: SKILLS FOR ENTERPRISE

*An exploration of The Big 13 enterprise skills as the foundation for any successful entrepreneurial venture*

## DAVID M GARBERA

First published 2012 by
Garbera Enterprise Ltd
141 Fairfax Avenue
Hull
HU5 4QZ
Tel 01482 445357


www.garberaenterprise.co.uk

ISBN 978-0-9561815-2-7

Printed in England by CPI Antony Rowe Ltd, Chippenham, Wiltshire

# Dedication

To the ambitious, the energetic and the enterprising

# Acknowledgements

My parents, particularly my dad, whose help, support and encouragement has been invaluable.

# Contents

# Foreword

AS an employer I strongly believe that young people today should be given the opportunity to acquire and develop employability skills.

RotherhamReady has led the way by developing The Big 13 to ensure that young people gain the skills required to be enterprising in life.

HullReady, as a Partner of RotherhamReady, has made available many opportunities to the young people of Hull.

I have been involved in the Make £5 Blossom campaign and witnessed young people using The Big 13 skills and I am constantly amazed to see how quickly the skills are grasped and utilised even at such a young age.

These qualities and skills will help bridge the gap between education and employment and equip young people for the future.

Dave Garbera is a shining example of this and in this, the third book of the trilogy he discusses The Big 13 Skills in turn, giving examples of how they have helped to shape his business and academic life.

*Vic Golding ACMA,*
*Managing Director,*
*Golding Computer Services Ltd, Hull.*

# Preface

SO here we are again! I am very pleased to be able to release the third instalment of the 'Smilers' trilogy. The final instalment, Skills for Enterprise, discusses the thirteen most important skills for success in any entrepreneurial venture. Step by step, I will break down each of these skills to explain, through my own experiences in business, how to get the best out of them and how they have helped me through the years. I am sure they will help you in exactly the same way. Starting a new business is easy – it's what happens afterwards that is tricky!

Building upon your initial idea and transforming it in to a successful and profitable business is not an overnight process. Time must be taken to build resources, reputation and, perhaps most importantly, confidence. The Big 13, adopted by Hull-Ready, will help to steer you in the right direction on your journey to becoming an entrepreneur. Developing these skills ensures all bases are covered when considering your next (or first!) move with a business idea. I feel strongly that these skills will point anyone considering starting their own enterprise towards triumph!

It is clear that young people today are more business minded than ever. Through the successes of programmes like Global Entrepreneurship Week, Youth Enterprise,  Make £5 Blossom and Young Enterprise, awareness of enterprise is at an all-time high. I hope the advice in this final book of the 'Smilers' trilogy will continue to offer constructive and valuable support in any venture. These are not just skills for business. They are skills for life.

Good luck!

*David M Garbera*
*Hull*
*November 2012*

# The Intro

STARTING a new business is not rocket science. It is, without a doubt, the easiest part of the whole business life cycle. No matter what the product or service on offer, virtually anyone can do it. Moreover, with the help of one of the many on-line companies (and a small fee) you can even have your own limited company up and running in a matter of hours. No, starting up the business is not the problem. The problem is growing that new business in to something that is both sustainable and profitable.

Over the last eight years or so I have met and talked with scores of successful business people. Hailing from all parts of the United Kingdom and representing a wide range of business interests, it was always quick and easy to spot their differences. Age, gender and a host of physical attributes rapidly marked them out as unique individuals. On the other hand, any similarities they shared were never quite so immediately obvious, and as a result took me a little longer to pin-point. Eventually, however, the penny dropped and I realised that without exception all of my business contacts appeared to share two things: first, a set of three very important personal qualities, namely, **ambition**, **energy** and **enterprise**, and second, a strong desire to acquire and develop a particular set of essential **business skills** – The Big 13 (RotherhamReady).

Moreover, this realisation finally dispelled any lingering doubts in my own mind that the role of luck, good or bad, had anything at all to do with their success. Winning the lottery may well be down to luck, but running a successful business is certainly not!

The idea of 'luck' is a very powerful concept in our society. If I had just a penny for every time the word was mentioned I would be a multi-millionaire. For instance, we wish people 'good luck' when taking an exam or going for an interview or entering some kind of competitive event. Conversely, we commiserate with people when something goes wrong in their lives or when they have been unsuccessful in achieving a particular goal, by placing the blame fairly and squarely on a random piece of 'bad luck'. We even claim that there are people who are born 'lucky' because they appear to achieve everything they want in life with little difficulty, whilst others whose lives appear to be blighted in some way can be simply dismissed as being 'unlucky'.

But for me, the whole idea of some mysterious and intangible force, lying in wait to influence my life in general or my business interests in particular, for good or ill, is totally unrealistic. Individual success is earned by acquiring the skills and knowledge appropriate to the task. In business, it enables the right decision to be taken at the right time. On the other hand, the price for being unprepared or for simply standing still, is the slippery slope towards failure. Never taking your eye off the ball is far more important in this context than any element of luck. Successful people don't need to appeal to 'lady luck' to get ahead, they make their own. And they make their own by making sure that they have the skills to support their, ambition, energy and enterprise.

All I will admit to is this. Sometimes an individual can, by accident or simple coincidence, find themselves 'in the right place, at the right time'. If you want to call that 'luck', then so be it. But, in my opinion, this circumstance can only be applied to such a small percentage of cases, that 'luck', in all seriousness, cannot be included as a factor in business success.

# Ambition, Energy and Enterprise

According to the Concise Oxford Dictionary, '**ambition**' is defined as 'an ardent desire for distinction; aspiration; object of such desire.' '**Energy**' as 'force, vigour (of speech, action or person); active operation; individual powers in use; latent ability', and '**enterprise**' as 'an undertaking, especially bold or difficult; business, firm; courage, readiness to engage in enterprises'.

A lot to digest all at once, but to my mind the whole thing can be boiled down in to three quite straightforward statements; one, **a strong desire to achieve**; two, **a willingness to work very hard** and three, **having the confidence to be creative and take a risk.**

People with ambition do not simply wish they could own a business – they go ahead and develop the business, even at the risk of failure. It is what drives the individual to achieve and continue to achieve as new and ever more challenging targets are set. Motivation and inspiration are fuelled by ambition. Without them success in business would be impossible. These are the qualities that stop us from simply drifting aimlessly with the tide. Instead, they provide clarity of purpose and the determination to achieve both short term and long term business goals.

Motivation is important because it is the strong, driving force that can mean the difference between failure and success. It is what helps to keep you going when ploughing through a boring task or during particularly demanding or stressful trading times.

Inspiration is what keeps you moving towards your goals. If you lose interest, you lose motivation and this can be a negative on your business. On the other hand when you are excited about what you are doing, your energy and motivation levels can go through the roof. So be honest with yourself. Does your business or business idea really inspire you? If it does not, then you may find it especially difficult to keep going during the challenging stages that every business, large or small, invariably goes through. Moreover, by setting long term and short term business goals you are more able to keep focussed and on track. I strongly believe that writing them down in a business plan is essential. You will be surprised to discover how much perspective you can achieve from goals, strategies and deadlines once they have been written down. This will give you the impetus needed to accomplish all of your targets. Equally, make sure that you remain on course by reviewing your goals honestly and frequently throughout the year.

Those without real energy hope to make it rich or to reach their goals by taking an easy path, but as soon as the path gets a little bumpy they give up and begin to seek a new path, or new goals. Blissfully unaware that nothing in life that's worth achieving comes without some personal cost, they never reach any of their goals.

High energy levels, on the other hand, show in your posture, your walk and your eyes. It projects enthusiasm and a drive to produce and succeed. An energetic person believes in the importance of hard work and the necessity of completing anything undertaken. Not surprisingly, there is little concern with the number of hours worked and no suggestion of 'clock watching'. In short, they possess what many would call a 'strong work ethic'.

Whatever your chosen field of business, you must be passionate about what you are trying to achieve and work as hard as you can to get ahead, to be successful. Giving up is never an option. But this requires the right attitude, self-discipline and, on occasion, the ability to put your business goals before your own needs. It's all about having the determination to keep trying, to keep struggling and, as a result, to overcome any and all obstacles that are put in your way. If you are actually serious about wanting to achieve your business goals there is no substitute for working hard.

The good thing about working hard is that people with high energy levels don't see it that way. They appear to enjoy what they do and, consequently, the work does not seem unduly gruelling. Working smartly helps, too. An intelligent working technique, along with relentless effort can go a long way in helping achieve success.

Enterprise means always finding a way to keep yourself actively working toward your ambition. It's about creativity and it's about having the courage to be creative. You need creativity to see what's out there and to shape it to your advantage. You need it to look at the world a little differently; to actually be different. Similarly, you need courage to see things from an alternative perspective, to go against the crowd, to take a different approach.

To be enterprising is all about keeping your eyes open and your mind active. It's about making your own luck, regardless of what is happening in the economy. It's having the skills, confidence and discipline to seize any opportunity that presents itself. A person with an enterprising attitude is someone who looks forward and not backward, someone that is always prepared for the bumpy road ahead.

As a result, an enterprising person is innovative and imaginative, an optimist and not a pessimist. It is someone who is highly motivated, energetic and has a capacity for hard work. They are busy, driven, dynamic and highly committed to getting things done. Their high motivation levels can be seen in their need for achievement, which, more often than not, is clearly demonstrated by a strong desire to lead and be involved. They don't wait for opportunities to come their way, instead they go after the opportunities, constantly seeking information and expertise to evaluate potential and assess risk. They are extremely good at utilising resources.

And lastly, being enterprising is not just about making huge sums of money. Being enterprising also means feeling good about yourself, and having enough self-belief to want to seek advantages and opportunities that will make a difference to your future. And by doing so, you will increase your confidence, your courage and your creativity; and by default your enterprising nature.

So what does all this tell you about being successful in the world of business? Well for a start, it means taking a long, hard (and honest) look at yourself, because for me, maintaining and growing a successful business has as much to do with the individual's personal qualities as it does with the product or service being provided. Equally, you need to realise that there are no short cuts. Hard work, complimented with a strong desire to acquire and develop a particular set of essential business skills, is the only sure way of reaching the sort of success that you might be aspiring to. Moreover, it is just as important to remember, and to believe, that once you combine ambition, energy and enterprise with your own individual talents there is nothing 'out there' that can defeat you!

# One of Thirteen

**Team Work**: The degree to which a group of people can work together effectively can be a decisive factor in whether they can achieve their goals. Much of good team work comes down to how well people get on with each other and their ability to apply basic social skills to get the best out of others and their situation. These skills include flexibility, sensitivity, compromise, persuasion, respecting and participating. With these skills a group can commit to a common purpose and attain their goals, they can act as effective mentors and nurture the best in one another.

**HullReady**

IN hindsight, one of the best decisions I ever made was to join a struggling Year 10 Young Enterprise group, called KH Smilers. However, in the autumn of 2003 when I was just 15 years old, I wasn't quite so sure that I had done the right thing. Up to that point I had never really considered myself as a serious team player. Over time, I had convinced myself that I did not have the desire, the ability, or the resolve to work as part of a team. What is more, the personal benefits of such an arrangement were at best unclear and at worst, irrelevant.

As a young person, in or out of school, I always preferred

individual pursuits to organised team games. I was much more comfortable relying on myself rather than on others to achieve a positive result. Moreover, I didn't want the pressure or the responsibility of others relying on me for their collective success. Letting a team down because of an incompetent act or a poor decision on my part was a scenario I preferred to avoid. So, for many years, I did just that.

Mind you, I needn't have worried. The more observant amongst you may have noticed that in my opening paragraph I referred to KH Smilers as a 'group' rather than a 'team'. This was a deliberate and considered choice on my part, for as I think back, it seems the most appropriate term to use. For, the one thing that the 'eighteen' were most definitely not, was a team.

When I came in as the new Sales Director (in November 2003) the company was, literally, being torn apart. Instead of working together to achieve a common purpose, some of the 18 directors and staff appeared to be doing exactly the opposite. 'Sides' would often be taken, usually based on friendship groups rather than on business goals and, as a result, meetings in particular started in a hostile atmosphere, then descended in to a chaotic free for all and subsequently ended with a handful of resignations. Clearly, a situation that could not last for long! And it didn't. By the New Year (2004) I was the Managing Director, the business had a new product and the company was down to six members, with only two of the original 'Smilers' surviving the cull. Now, we had the opportunity to start from scratch and strive to become a real Young Enterprise team.

I cannot overstate how important it is for any individual to be able to work as part of a team, to be in some way a team player. None of us live in a vacuum or in total isolation on a desert island and, therefore, to a greater or lesser degree, we all need to develop the skill of working with others. However, in business I believe it is absolutely essential. To my mind, any entrepreneurial venture will require the hearts and minds of several people, all pulling in the same direction, if the desired outcome – a successful business - is to be achieved. Unfortunately, like many things in life, this is sometimes easier said than done.

For me and the new KH Smilers it started with a Mission statement. Some form of words that we could all subscribe to, and that would subsequently act as a constant personal reminder of what the business was trying to achieve.

*"We at KH Smilers aim and strive to provide quality bedding plants and above all excellent service to all customers and clients, while also **maintaining a friendly working atmosphere** within the company."*

After my previous experience with the original business I felt that it was particularly important to include something about our personal relationships within the company (highlighted above). The implication was obvious. We had to work and behave as a team. And I can honestly say that by and large we did!

Implementing a new company structure (Appendix 1), with each director having clearly defined roles and responsibilities strengthened our new found spirit of co-operation. Written in such a way as to make them manageable and acceptable to the whole team, we could, as a result, avoid long pointless arguments over who should do what and when. Efficiency would be maximised, errors reduced and chaos avoided. A clear recipe for success!

But even though there were only six of us we still held a secret ballot to allocate the positions in the company. After a short period of discussion, each of us decided which of the eight directorships would suit us best. Then, with voting slips and a small box at hand, it was time to hold the election.

The procedure took very little time and within minutes each of us were individually returned (in our preferred roles) with a unanimous vote. More importantly, this transparent and democratic procedure ensured that there would be no recriminations or petty squabbles after the election process.

Next, I turned my thoughts to the conduct of Board Meetings. In the past such meetings had always been, to put it politely, rather topsy-turvy affairs. More importantly, you didn't need to be Einstein to spot the major problem. Very simply, as people entered the meeting room, most of them seemed to throw their basic social skills out of the window. For a short period of time the 'law of the jungle' seemed to take over, and the participants were more than willing to become 'red in tooth and claw'. A clear recipe for disaster!

Fortunately, the solution was as simple as identifying the core problem – a set of rules that would guide our behaviour and so enable meetings to be positive, productive and business-like (Appendix 2). These were discussed and eventually agreed to by us all. However, let me make it absolutely clear that this was never an attempt on my part to dominate or to manipulate the Board-room, and so stifle the freedom of individuals to express their views. No, it was always about creating an atmosphere where everyone would feel valued and able to contribute without the fear of being bullied or ridiculed by more confident and possibly more aggressive personalities. And, in essence it worked. Each of us was fully aware of our individual responsibilities in maintaining a healthy and purposeful atmosphere during meetings. This meant listening to and respecting each other's opinions; showing a measure of sensitivity when addressing the needs of other team members; being transparent and open to persuasion, as well as displaying a genuine willingness to compromise. Sticking to the rules brought out the best in each of us and allowed us to remain friends as well as colleagues. Chairing the meetings was, therefore, always a doddle – well, nearly always!

Although having these rules did not guarantee trouble free

meetings or the odd outburst, I can truthfully say that by collectively adhering to them, any disruption was kept to an absolute minimum. And in no way was anybody ever harmed by the process of enforcement!

Our team spirit was further reinforced by the six of us agreeing to be flexible, and work on as many tasks as possible together. Obviously we each had our own responsibilities within the company, but the general feeling was that there were lots of opportunities for co-operation and  sharing that did not directly involve treading on someone else's toes. This was especially true of the production process, as this was not the preserve of one particular company director. Here, we could all have a go at a range of different tasks including sowing seeds, potting on seedlings in to their appropriate trays and planting up tubs and hanging baskets. Some of our efforts, especially in the more creative aspects of the work, were indeed quite comical. But the important thing was that we laughed **with** each other and not **at** each other. These were ideal opportunities to offer encouragement, help, advice and support without being patronising or sarcastic. It brought us closer together. It helped us to become a team.

By the time the YE Company Programme competition began in earnest (April 2004), KH Smilers had been transformed in to a completely different beast, unrecognisable from the one that started life in the previous September. We had, in my opinion, become a force to be reckoned with, a formidable team. Realising that our strength was in our togetherness, we bore witness to the old saying 'united we stand, divided we fall'. The newly created team spirit shone through like a Ready Brek glow. The company was, at last, pulling together in the same direction to achieve our common business goals. The importance of working as a team had been recognised, embraced, developed and put in to practice by us all. Without it, KH Smilers would have been doomed to failure for the second time in its very short existence. As a result, progress as a business or in the YE competition would have been impossible. Indeed, it was this skill that provided the firm foundations for everything else to develop. It was both the catalyst and the springboard for all our future success.

For me, this was a particularly important moment, as in just a few short weeks I had become what I had convinced myself I was not – a team player. There was now no doubt in my own mind that I had the ability and the resolve to work with others to achieve both short and long term goals. Moreover, the importance of maintaining and honing this essential skill has stayed with me ever since. In fact I wouldn't be where I am today without it!

In addition, once the YE phase of the company disappeared in to the ether, four of the team including myself, felt that we could continue to work together. Knowing and accepting each other's strengths and weaknesses made this team even stronger. Bringing all our shared experience and learning to the venture gave us the strength to take on the real world of business, and prove that coming from a comprehensive school, and being just fifteen years of age, was NOT a handicap to success. In fact, in my view, carrying those labels had the exact opposite effect. Rather than proving to be a major hurdle in the race for recognition, those two particular attributes made us more resilient, and even more determined to overcome such misguided perceptions. Clearly, it wasn't going to happen overnight. It would take time and lots of hard work on our part, but then, nothing comes for free!

# What Can You Do?

| | | | | | |
|---|---|---|---|---|---|
| **TEAM WORK** | | | | | |
| **Beginner** | **Phase 1** | **Phase 2** | **Phase 3** | **Phase 4** | **Expert** |
| I know why team work is important | I can work in a team and share | I know how my strengths fit into a team | I know how others strengths fit into a team | I can evaluate how my team works | I can use previous learning to improve my team |

**(Developed by RotherhamReady as partners of HullReady)**

# Two of Thirteen

**Risk Management:** What is risk?   A hazard?   A misfortune?  The possibility of losing?  The possibility of failing?    Contemplating any of these seemingly negative outcomes could put a person off taking action if success is not a given.  However, learning to cope with and manage risk is imperative for anyone who wants to progress in life.  Managing risk is the process of identifying different threats and possibilities and seeing how they can be mitigated, controlled or simply accepted.  But learning to manage risk develops the confidence to take informed decisions which can turn risks into opportunities.                **HullReady**

FOR many years of my life, 'Risk' was nothing more than an entertaining strategic board game where each player struggles against his or her opponents for world domination!  Little to do with reality, it would while away many a happy hour during school holidays and at weekends.   Or so I thought.   It never dawned on me until much later on that, in fact, the decisions I made during the game and the opportunities that I created as a result, mirrored processes in real life almost exactly.   The only significant difference being that the consequence of any decision, good or bad, was confined to the imaginary world of the game. Even so, I was still very cautious.  I was what you might call risk averse. Dodgy, untried or untested strategies led to mistakes and mistakes meant losing. And I didn't like to lose! Unfortunately, it also meant that I didn't win very often either. To do that you had to take a risk.

Looking back, I simply did not understand that taking a risk and making mistakes could actually provide excellent opportunities for learning. To my young mind, mistakes equated to failure. In the imaginary world of 'Risk' I don't suppose it really mattered, but in the real world of day to day living and learning, it proved to be a major failing, and one that I didn't really overcome until I joined KH Smilers.

Indeed, that one simple act of joining a company teetering on the edge of oblivion, proved to be my first truly risky business decision. With my previous track record for being cautious and avoiding failure, I should have unhesitatingly declined the offer and walked away. But I didn't. Even to this day I am uncertain as to why. Maybe it's because the company was already so close to folding, that if the worst should happen I could stand back as the new boy, absolve myself of blame and point the finger at everybody else. On the other hand, I prefer to believe it had more to do with age, with growing up, and having the emotional maturity to take on board the possible negative outcomes of taking such a risk. Either way, I accepted the risk and, with my fellow directors took on the challenge of saving KH Smilers. A challenge that demanded, both as a team and as individuals, we devise and implement one risky strategy after another. I haven't looked back since.

There can be little doubt that when I took over the reins of KH Smilers success was far from assured. In fact, the chances of the whole thing going 'belly up' were very real. Let me just recap the situation for you, review the 'pros' and 'cons'. I'll start with the 'pros' because that's easy. There aren't any. And as far as the 'cons' are concerned, where do I start? No immediately saleable product, £250 in debt, creditors forcefully demanding to be paid, a mountain of essentially useless unsold stock, a Boardroom in disarray and a slimmed down team of just six. An outsider could easily be forgiven for thinking that a snowball in hell probably had a better chance of survival than we did. But whatever the outcome, this set of circumstances had to be managed, and had to be managed quickly.

However, we did have one very powerful weapon in our arsenal – team spirit. Combined with a steely resolve to be successful, the risks we took were not frivolous but calculated. And that made all the difference to the rapid change around in the fortunes of the company.

First of all we had to accept that the old KH Smilers was dead. Obviously, lessons had been learned but we had to move on. Crying over spilt milk or constantly wringing our hands and wailing over the situation we were in, was never an option. On the other hand quickly agreeing a new product certainly was. But it couldn't be any old product or service. It had to be one that stood a good chance of clearing our massive debt first and then going on to make us a healthy profit. And summer bedding plants was my answer. Once identified, this product had all the hallmarks of being able to do exactly what we required of it. Even though the market research (an ideal tool for assessing risk) was, out of necessity, somewhat rushed, the conclusions totally vindicated our choice of growing and selling summer bedding plants. There was only one potential threat, pest infestation and disease. Fortunately, we readily accepted that this might be a problem but also realised that with careful husbandry and expert advice this risk was entirely manageable. In any event, it was highly unlikely that we would lose all of our plants.

Deciding on how best to advertise and market our plants could not be left for long either. Growing the plants was one thing, getting rid of them was another. The success of KH Smilers hinged on getting this right, first time. Our existence had to be brought to the attention of the local community as soon as possible. After all this would be our market place for potential customers. Time was of the essence, orders had to be taken. Moreover, by allowing our plants to be pre-ordered we could avoid overspending and over-stocking. A strategy our predecessors clearly failed to consider, never mind put in to practice. But for us it proved to be a stroke of genius. With no money changing hands until the order was delivered our customers knew that they were in no danger of losing their investment. For them it was a risk free transaction. The worst that could happen is that no plants would be forth-coming, and they would have to go elsewhere. As a result, obtaining the orders we required was less of a problem than we might have imagined.

In a matter of days, opportunities for raising capital had also been identified and implemented, flyers and order forms had been printed, a website was under construction and our attendance at a variety of school Parents' Evenings had been arranged and confirmed. The basics for a successful re-launch were in place. At this stage, I was as confident as I could be that decisions had been well informed and that any future potential risks were entirely manageable and most definitely under our control. True, failure was still a possibility, but that fact alone did not stop us from taking the actions necessary to secure the immediate and long term success of KH Smilers. In the end it was all about balance, and I believe we got it absolutely right!

Having learned a great deal about business and myself from participating in the YE competition, taking KH Smilers forward as a limited company held no fear for me. I knew the product, the market and the customers. All the spade work had already been done. There was none of the apprehension involved when entering a new market, and as a result I knew that any investment would be absolutely safe, or as safe as anything in this world can be. Suffice to say the risk had been calculated and minimised to the best of my ability. This was equally true of each decision made to expand capacity or diversify in to new plants and services. For example, deciding to offer a winter range of plants and free delivery could have had negative financial consequences for the business but I was not scared of trying something new. If it failed I would learn from it!

The story is similar with Garbera Enterprise. The risk free option would have been to find a commercial Publisher. In one swift move the risk is shifted from the author to the publisher. If the book flops it is the Publisher who takes the hit. The author, on the other hand, has the satisfaction of seeing the book in print and on the bookshelves but avoids any of the costs. Unfortunately, obtaining such a book deal is very difficult. Therefore, after doing the market research, and speaking to potential customers I was convinced that the demand for a series of 'Smilers' books was big enough to risk the expense of self-publishing. With no real experience in this area there was always a significant risk that I could get things horribly wrong. But by taking the time to do the research and establish my exact costs, I knew exactly what the financial risk would be. At this point the fear of failure could have put me off but instead I accepted that I had done everything possible to limit any possible damage and took the decision to go ahead. And as the sales for Book 1 and Book 2 have reached nearly two thousand, I feel fully vindicated that the decision to press ahead was the right one. In addition, even though I have borne all the costs, I haven't had to share any profits with an outside Publisher. This made investment in the trilogy so much easier.

## What Can You Do?

| | | | | | |
|---|---|---|---|---|---|
| **RISK** | | | | | |
| **Beginner** | **Phase 1** | **Phase 2** | **Phase 3** | **Phase 4** | **Expert** |
| I am willing to try new activities | I understand that trying new things is taking a risk | I don't let the thought of failure put me off | I have the confidence to take calculated risks | I can decide which risks can be heeded, reduced or accepted | I use failure as a way of learning what to do differently next time |

**(Developed by RotherhamReady as partners of HullReady)**

# Three of Thirteen

**Negotiating And Influencing**: People spend a lot of time and effort trying to persuade each other to do what *they* want, whether in personal or professional situations. Effective negotiation requires a high level of communication, the ability to build rapport and persuade rationally, and the confidence to deal with 'difficult' situations that could be a block to success. Negotiating and influencing also encompasses the ability to listen and compromise. It includes the ability to be turned down, knocked back but still to participate.

**HullReady**

SITUATIONS that require people to work together for a common purpose have the capacity to become problematic. Beneath the surface, tension, with its potential for destructive conflict, is always a possibility. Let's face it, even the best of friends can sometimes fall out over the most trivial of reasons! But it is the inability to manage or resolve conflict that, in the longer term, causes all the damage. Tension within a group is normal. After all, as individuals we all bring different personalities, attitudes, skills and views to the table. However, properly harnessed such diversity can bring innovation and creativity to any venture, but if allowed to fester and spiral out of control the potential for unhealthy and damaging conflict is great.

As a society and as individuals, we are constantly being bombarded, 24/7, by an advertising industry that has managed to permeate every aspect of our daily lives. In the hope of influencing our decisions and/or opinions in some way these professional 'persuaders' have managed to generate a multi-million pound business. Whether this is done via the radio, TV, Internet or printed media the results can be instant and powerful.

Be that as it may, persuading or influencing others is not the preserve of the advertisers. For good or ill it is a normal part of everyday life and something we all experience from an early age. From shouting and threatening to coaxing and bribery, the techniques used to make us take a particular course of action are many and varied. Indeed, I am sure you can think of dozens of examples from your own lives that have involved some or all of these approaches. Nonetheless, I can't resist just one example. It comes from a TV advert.

Mother and son are shopping in a supermarket. Son picks up an item he wants. Mother refuses to buy. Son immediately throws himself to the floor kicking and screaming. Putting aside her trolley mother's response is to do exactly the same. Gobsmacked, son stands up, looks on in total disbelief and returns the item. Mother follows suit and gets to her feet. With a nod of her head they move on. Conflict resolved the advert ends.

Alright, funny and extreme as it may be, the mother's way of persuading her son to do as she wanted would not suit us all. The important lesson here is, just like the advertisers, we should all recognise that the twin skills of persuasion and influencing are valuable assets in our personal armouries. Therefore, to spend time understanding and developing them is never going to be a waste.

In every group of people, large or small, some people seem to have more influence than others. Moreover, people with influence seem to affect what happens more than other people do. The reasons for this are undoubtedly many and varied but could easily include things like being assertive, clever, funny, honest, popular and/or different. But it is how we use this skill, rather than simply possessing it, that is so important. For instance, whilst the majority will use this skill in a positive way to help and support or to resolve difficult situations, a minority will deliberately seek to gain some personal advantage from any given situation by exerting a bad or negative influence on those around them.

Although I can't be sure, this is what I have come to believe may have happened within the original KH Smilers. Regrettably, at that time there was no one in the company who was able to challenge the negativity of a few, and so their influence was allowed to spread, until it affected and then engulfed the majority, thus forcing, in quick succession, the resignations of the least resilient.

Even so, what was also missing was someone within the group who could, in some way, negotiate with and then persuade those who might have still been willing to listen, to acknowledge the problems they faced and so embark on a more positive course of action. Neither did anyone appear to have the confidence or strength of will to build the bridges necessary to get everyone to pull together and save the business. As a result, conflicts within the group remained unresolved and a difficult situation was simply allowed to grow worse and then, unsurprisingly, turn in to an almighty disaster. For this group, once the self- destruct button had been pushed there was no going back!

For me, on the other hand, coming in as the new Managing Director, there was no 'baggage', no legacy of conflict and disruption. As we returned to school in the January of 2004 the atmosphere within the new team was totally different. Slimmed down to one-third of the size – possibly an advantage - there was now a genuine feeling that we were all in this together. For better or for worse the new Board of Directors could now have a real go at saving KH Smilers.

With our new found optimism we soon built up a rapport that allowed a climate of frank and honest discussion to develop. From now on bridges would not be burned but built. Talking and listening openly to each other became second nature.

Especially vital was the listening. Not the sort that mimicked a nodding dog yet, knowingly, allowing the message to go in one ear and then straight out of the other, but the sort that truly sought to understand the views or opinions being expressed by the speaker. As a result both individual and group conversations were nearly always based on rational argument rather than emotional rhetoric. Differing points of view were given equal consideration before any vote or decision was taken. In addition, it was accepted and understood that a majority resolution would always prevail.

That is not to say that the debate wasn't sometimes lively, heated or passionate. It was. After all, when people feel strongly about a particular situation it is only to be expected. The important thing was to keep the exchanges professional and not personal. No successful business has room for grudges, payback or self-indulgent recriminations. KH Smilers was no different.

However, having to compromise in some way by accepting a more persuasive or compelling argument, was never made to feel like an individual defeat or failure. Everyone had to be kept on board. Nobody was going to take their bat home this time around. Therefore, as long as we all kept an open mind and were, as individuals, willing to negotiate and/or be persuaded to move ground, difficult situations could be managed without any one of us feeling that our opinions had been simply swept aside or ignored altogether. The next day, any differences would be expected to be forgotten and it would be, as far as I was concerned, business as usual. Not that it always happened that way. I would be a liar if I said otherwise. So I'll simply have to face the truth. Just like all the other billions of people on this planet we are more sinners than saints!

# What Can You Do?

## NEGOTIATING AND INFLUENCING

| Beginner | Phase 1 | Phase 2 | Phase 3 | Phase 4 | Expert |
|---|---|---|---|---|---|
| I can give reasons for my ideas | I understand that not everyone will agree with my ideas | I can make a positive contribution to discussions | I am willing to commit to an idea that is not my own | I can persuade people to buy into and support my ideas | I can broker win-win agreements |

**(Developed by RotherhamReady as partners of HullReady)**

# Four of Thirteen

**Effective Communication**: This is an essential skill for life. From understanding the importance of first impressions to having the confidence to speak in meetings, from sending appropriate emails to making a connection with someone over the telephone – a high level of communication is essential. Acquiring and developing the necessary language skills (including new vocabulary) to express and present ideas to others is paramount.

**HullReady**

FOR as far back as I can remember the English language, in all of its forms, has been a passion of mine. Learning to talk gave me the voice I needed to express my needs, my emotions and my understanding of the world I lived in: learning to read opened the door to countless mysterious worlds, a myriad of new words and an endless supply of exciting experiences, whilst learning to write gave visual expression to my own creativity, my innermost thoughts and unexplored ideas. Therefore, quite honestly, communication in the broadest sense has never been a particular problem of mine.

However, one aspect of this essential skill that was most definitely out of my 'comfort zone' was the idea of 'presentation'. The thought of me standing, or even sitting come to that, in front of an audience, large or small, filled me with terror. What is more, the fact that my performance, in terms of the impending Young Enterprise competition, would be judged and assessed by panels of experts from the business community made it an even scarier prospect.

From my own limited business experience I have learned that developing effective channels of communication is essential. In fact I would go a stage further and say that an organisation without an efficient means of transmitting information is doomed to failure. This not only applies internally but also externally. It is just as important to establish a meaningful dialogue with the workforce as it is with customers. And as a Sales Director with the original KH Smilers I witnessed, at first hand, the destructive effects of poor communication on the company. As a result I was determined that the second incarnation of KH Smilers would not fall in to the same trap. Therefore, once we had agreed on a new product we focussed a lot of energy on devising positive ways of talking to each other as well as to our potential customers. Communication breakdown, at any level, was no longer an option!

As you already know a set of rules for the Boardroom were quickly agreed. This gave us the time and opportunity to give serious thought to other ways of keeping in touch with each other. The most obvious way was by telephone, particularly via our mobile phones. Not quite as versatile as today's vast range of iphones and associated 'apps', but it allowed for cheap on demand texting.

Another successful way of keeping an 'open channel' 24\7 was a staff message board on our KH Smilers web site. It meant that we could 'talk' to each other even though we were neither together nor in the same room. In addition, ideas to progress the business or items for the Boardroom agenda could be posted any time of day or night before they were forgotten. Personal emails could also be exchanged if a matter was individually sensitive or in need of some discretion.

In any event, whether we were talking on the telephone, texting or emailing, we were all acquiring and developing a whole new portfolio of useful language and communication skills – both for business and for life.

As far as our customers were concerned we were equally as determined and diligent to get things right. Apart from when we attended Parents' Evenings, first contact was normally via the letterbox. As a company we knew that to be successful in selling 3000 plants we had to target a wider market. It was, therefore, decided that we should put a leaflet and an order form in to an envelope and then deliver them to homes in the immediate area of the school. Many would have children at the school so would be more inclined to support us. Clearly, we ran the risk of targeting some people twice, but I believed that it was worth the gamble. Anyway, giving people a nudge with a second reminder was not such a bad thing. Businesses in the real world do it all the time!

The content was brief. Everything that we needed to say had to fit on one side of an A5 sheet. Choosing the right words, style and language was, therefore, paramount. Potential customers did not want to spend hours reading an essay on the company. All they needed to know was who we were, what we sold and how the product could be ordered (contact information). The actual order form would give more detail of plants, prices, method of payment and delivery time. Furthermore, for those customers who were interested and had access to the Internet, our web site provided everything that they would want to know. This was a read only web site. Once again, as with the flyers, our choice of words and language was very important.

I have already mentioned the telephone as a means of communicating with each other. This was also an important point of contact between KH Smilers and our customers. Indeed, if I am not mistaken, we received several orders this way especially from people who had heard of us by 'word of mouth', and so did not have access to an official order form. Moreover, during the month of May we would need to speak to all of our customers to arrange a mutually convenient delivery time.

Such important conversations I believed could not be left to chance. The quality, tone and manner of our telephone interactions had to be as professional as possible. I had no doubt in my mind that many of our customers might be inclined to judge the company by the way we spoke to them over the telephone. Therefore, for both scenarios, i.e. taking an order or arranging a delivery time, appropriate prompt cards were devised (Appendix 3). Having these cards also made the whole process less stressful for us. Admittedly, the first one or two calls we took as individuals proved to be a little nerve racking, but very quickly the prompts were committed to memory and everyone became much more relaxed with the whole idea of customer contact.

During this time KH Smilers also produced two newsletters (in May and June) for our customers and shareholders. Called 'Cuttings from the Greenhouse', it was our way of giving our supporters a flavour of the experiences we were having and an opportunity to feel part of the company that they had helped to make so successful. And judging by the feedback we received the newsletters went down really well.

The written word, however, was not our only means of communication. The spoken word was equally as important to our success. From networking with individual business men and women to company presentations in front of audiences large and small, our abilities in this field were constantly being put to the test.

Indeed, being only 14 or 15 years old, we soon realised that how we spoke to the members of the business community would largely determine how seriously they would take us. This was especially true once the company became KH Smilers Limited in the autumn of 2004. Believe me, first impressions really do count!

At each stage of our Young Enterprise journey we were expected to talk with both judges and general public alike. But the conversation was not the same. We were acutely aware that the language used with the judges had to be more formal, and reflect our understanding of the business processes that we were using. In many respects we had to learn a whole new vocabulary. Being unable to use the correct/precise words to describe our marketing or financial strategies for example, could suggest a possible lack of knowledge or understanding on our part. On the other hand, conversations with the public at large could be less formal and more 'chatty'. Without the element of being judged in some way the atmosphere was always going to be more relaxed.

Preparing for a presentation, however, was a different ball game altogether. Responding to a judge was out of necessity 'off the cuff'. Without having the specific questions beforehand it was impossible to prepare a stock answer. Clearly, we were aware of the criteria we would be judged against so, in one sense, we were prepared, but any individual responses would have to be mentally tailored to the specific question posed at the time. It was always about having the mental agility to think on your feet. Thankfully, this was a skill we practised regularly - simply by asking each other pertinent questions – and as a result, we are all quite good at.

We applied a similar technique to devising and delivering our presentation. The only major difference being that we had total and absolute control over what came out of our mouths. We knew what we had to say but how we said it was up to us!

Obviously, writing the script came first. This was a long, slow and, on occasion, painful process. Limited to 5 minutes and with a mountain of information to squeeze in, our abilities in this area would be repeatedly tested. Every word was carefully chosen and each sentence skilfully crafted. Paragraph after paragraph began to take shape. And after untold hours of deliberation and dare I say it argument, it was done. The KH Smilers company presentation was ready to be aired.

Rehearsals took place on several occasions, mostly behind closed doors but sometimes in front of a small audience. Under the pressure of trying to get it right tempers often flared and feet were regularly stamped. Constructive criticism wasn't always accepted in the spirit that it was given. However, step by painful step, we could see our performance becoming more proficient, more polished. By the time of the first presentation we were as confident as we could be that the team performance would be good. And it was. Otherwise, I am sure KH Smilers would not have got through to the next round of the competition.

Throughout, we continued to work on our presentation. Although we tweaked the script and PowerPoint here and there, essentially it stayed the same. It was simply a matter of updating certain aspects of the company profile, for instance, finance and sales. On the other hand, our performance continued to develop and change. The more we rehearsed the more confidence we displayed in our delivery. By the time of our final outing at the Savoy Hotel in London (Appendix 4), we were like a well-oiled machine, slick and professional throughout. And, in my humble opinion, gave our much older counterparts a serious run for their money.

Since those days I have prepared and delivered umpteen presentations to a whole range of audiences – from school children and students, to high profile members of the business community. Although, like anyone, I can get a little nervous, the nerves never detract from the performance. No matter what the occasion, I have the utmost confidence in my own ability to present information that is relevant to the people in front of me, and in a way that will engage and hold their interest.

I should also mention that good communication skills are essential when dealing with the media, whether that is the press, the radio or the television. As it happens I have never been interviewed for mainstream television (my one experience was with an Internet TV channel), but my companies or I have featured many times in the press and occasionally on the radio. The important thing to remember is that although this type of publicity is free you will have little editorial control. So remember, listen to the questions carefully and think before you speak, but take the opportunity to get your message across. In most cases you can then use the publicity received in your own advertising and marketing strategies. However, always check for copyright and get permission if required.

# What Can You Do?

## EFFECTIVE COMMUNICATION

| Beginner | Phase 1 | Phase 2 | Phase 3 | Phase 4 | Expert |
|----------|---------|---------|---------|---------|--------|
| I can listen effectively to others | I can talk to people I know | I can communicate effectively in familiar groups | I understand the importance of non-verbal communication | I listen, filter information and respond appropriately | I can speak to different audiences and maintain their interest |

(Developed by RotherhamReady as partners of HullReady)

# Five of Thirteen

**Creativity And Innovation**: These skills can be seen in a number of ways – the generation of ideas and concepts, making things or even taking a new approach to a familiar activity. It is about being imaginative – thinking 'outside the box' – looking for solutions, solving problems, inventing new ideas. And then imagining that something 'extra' which will be the spark for innovation or improvement.

**HullReady**

PROBLEMS within a business can often bring people together and induce both creativity and innovation. Unfortunately, this did not happen with the first incarnation of KH Smilers. Indeed, the reaction of its members was virtually the exact opposite – divisions became deeper and the majority of the group voted with their feet and walked away. Resignations reached epidemic proportions and the company collapsed like a house of cards. Only then, in a last ditch bid to save the company did a new Board of Directors bring both creativity and innovation to the table and allowed them to truly blossom. Within days, like the Phoenix, a new and shiny KH Smilers began to rise from the ashes of the old.

As I opened the first meeting as Managing Director my overriding concern was to find a new product or service for the company to sell. Easier said than done I know, but I was determined to find something that could help us to move forward as a business. For a variety of reasons all of the Ideas the team had considered just before the Christmas break were quickly discounted. They all had flaws or problems that we were unable to solve in the time that we had left to get ready for the YE competition (about 12 weeks). Silence descended as we racked our brains for something new. Not 'new' in the sense that it had never been done before, but something that allowed the company to enter a market that was still relatively competition free. An area, as newcomers, we would have a decent chance of being successful.

It was at this point that I had my 'eureka' moment, a brief but inspirational excursion 'outside the box'. Remembering a conversation that I had recently had , I tabled the idea that we could grow and sell bedding plants for the coming summer season. Not only that, we would provide a complete service by delivering orders to the door. Moreover, if we did not ask for payment until the plants were successfully delivered, the transaction for the customer would be completely risk free. The worse that could happen is that they would have to buy their plants in the same way as they had done in previous years. In addition, I couldn't think of any other business in the local area providing such a service. To all intents and purposes I had spotted a gap in the market, a niche that we could occupy and exploit.

As my proposal slowly sunk in, and with no other credible ideas on the table, I moved that we took a vote. One by one the hands went up. Besides my own I counted five. It was unanimous. KH Smilers would no longer be selling a range of novelty items but instead a selection of summer bedding plants. As a group united in purpose, we had chosen a product that everyone was happy with. This was indeed a significant step forward on our planned route to recovery. One problem solved but many more to go!

Whether as part of the YE Company Programme competition or

as an exhibitor at an organised Trade Fair, I always took the view that our trade stand was an integral part of showcasing who we were, and what we were selling. It was a visual representation of what we were all about, and, to boot, a fantastic opportunity to unleash our creative talents. As a result, spending time, effort and money on getting this just right was never going to be a waste. In my opinion, it could only enhance our credibility and increase the prospects of KH Smilers becoming a successful business.

Designing and continually updating an ever evolving trade stand created a lot of healthy debate within the team. When it came to the aesthetics we all had an opinion, valid or otherwise. But we all took a strong interest in the creative process. Working individually and sometimes together, several possible designs were committed to paper and then discussed in detail by the whole team. We all needed to understand and be happy with the final choice. The only limiting factors were our own imaginations and, of course, our greatest enemy, space. Every event we attended prescribed exactly the area that KH Smilers could occupy.

At York (Venturefest 2004), we set to work in our allocated space as soon as everything had been brought in and unpacked. To the top of each display board we pinned a large laminated banner, clearly identifying the stand as belonging to KH Smilers. Directly underneath, and imaginatively positioned, various examples of our marketing materials (posters, flyers, order forms); photographs and job descriptions of each of the six directors, as well as detailed product information. On the table I set up the laptop. Any visitor to the stand could use this to browse the KH Smilers website or access a range of company information. To either side of the computer screen, priced and ready for sale, Whacky Test Tubes and planted terracotta pots. Finally, to encourage visitors to come to our stand I put out a mouth-watering bowl of sweets, and organised a free, no tickets required, raffle. Everyone who visited our stand simply popped their business card in to a container. The prize, a large decorative pot that we had planted up, would then be independently drawn just before the end of the day. What could be easier? But even better, the business cards provided us with a ready-made list of contacts!

Next, we turned all our attention towards the YE Company Programme. As an important element of the competition, the trade stand was used on a further five occasions, but at least now, we could concentrate on our main business – summer bedding plants for borders, hanging baskets and containers. Unfortunately, this resulted in more work for the team as a new overall design was needed to reflect this significant change. Once more, however, we felt that simplicity was the key. Several brainstorming sessions later, and mindful of the fact that our plants needed to be at the heart of the display, a design began to evolve that met the five main criteria that we had set ourselves at the start of the process, namely, that the stand had to be functional, informative, effective, aesthetically pleasing and relatively inexpensive. And what finally emerged ticked all the boxes.

Therefore, at the KC Stadium and Barton we would concentrate on recreating a scene familiar to any gardener or family throughout the country. In the centre was a large garden umbrella. Beneath it, a table covered in artificial grass on which were displayed order forms, KH Smilers flyers, a laptop running company information, small items of garden equipment (trowel, fork, secateurs, etc) and a large seductive bowl of sweets. To the left and right familiar garden tools – wheel barrow, spade, garden fork, rake, edging sheers and so on. Round the back, and carefully positioned so as not to look too cluttered, company name/logo, posters advertising our products and large photographs of the team at work in the greenhouses. Then the whole area was liberally sprinkled with trays of bedding plants and a range of our colourfully planted decorative pots. Pretty as a picture!

Unfortunately, an award for the trade stand eluded us on both occasions, so before going on to the regional final in Sheffield it was back to the drawing board. Fortunately our creative juices were still flowing, and within no time at all we were exploring a host of new, exciting ideas. As a result a much improved design was soon unveiled. It became the blueprint for the next KH Smilers trade stand, used both at Sheffield and the UK final in London.

The table covered in artificial grass remained but the umbrella was ditched. Instead, the table was enclosed by three large trellis panels carefully hinged together. The whole framework was then locked together by using a fourth arched panel screwed across the top. This carried the company name, KH Smilers. Each letter of the name had been made from bright yellow artificial flowers and carefully pinned in to place. Finally, the whole area was dressed with photographs, previous awards, posters, newsletters, laptop, hanging baskets, colourful terracotta pots and loads of summer bedding plants. Subtle lighting completed the picture. The final result on both occasions was, in my opinion, magnificent. Sadly, an individual award for the best trade stand was not being given at either of the two events. Pity!

Another area that demanded a creative input was the KH Smilers website. A brainstorming session produced a design we were all happy with as well as a transcript of the contents, including pictures. This was not a shop as such (that came later when the company went limited) but a read only site, where any of our potential customers with access to the Internet could find out more about us and our plants. Probably quite an amateur affair by today's standards, but we did everything ourselves and the final result certainly showed that we had the ability to create an informative as well as a visually exciting experience. So, with the aid of a free downloaded template and a hosting service, the KH Smilers website went live very quickly.

Finally, we put our minds to the design of the fliers, order form and newsletters. The brief we gave ourselves was very straightforward. The flyer should be simple but eye catching; the content brief. Everything that we needed to say had to fit on one side of an A5 sheet. Potential customers did not want to spend hours reading an essay on the company. All they needed to know was who we were; what we sold and how the product could be ordered (contact information). The order form should be simple, uncluttered and easy to fill in; essential information would include name, address and telephone number of the customer, type of plants for sale, prices, method of payment and delivery time. Minimalist but highly effective would describe both finished products. In clear black and white, they did 'exactly what it said on the tin'. The newsletter on the other hand should be glossy, colourful and reflect success, the printed version of a human 'show off'! Indeed, the use of colour was to be one of the most important design features of our newsletter, 'Cuttings from the Greenhouse'. As well as being informative we wanted each one to be a visual feast. And they were!

When I incorporated Garbera Enterprise, I could bring all my creative experiences with KH Smilers to the world of publishing. As a first time self-publisher I simply could not afford to buy in the expertise of an illustrator or a graphic designer. The bottom line was easily drawn. It was all down to me.

An illustration for the front cover was first. As the title for the book was 'From the Ashes', the most appropriate illustration, as far as I was concerned, would be that of a Phoenix rising out of a fire. I hunted for one on the Internet. Before long I found a magnificent illustration drawn by an artist in the USA. As it was a copyright image I emailed her to negotiate a fee for its use. Unfortunately, after an exchange of emails it transpired that this illustration had already been used in another book, and to untangle the different claims on the image would have been very difficult and possibly very expensive. The hunt was on again. Within minutes I had found another illustration. Not quite as good as the first but for a fee of £8 I had unlimited use of the image. Deal done, I set about completing the remainder of the design, including sourcing a picture of myself for the back cover. Pictures for the body of the book were also found and placed. Although I would have liked them in colour, the costs were prohibitive and, therefore, I had to settle for black and white. For Books 2 and 3 I decided to produce my own photographic images for the front covers. This avoided the thorny question of copyright and was essentially free.

Web shops for KH Smilers (www.khsmilers.co.uk) and Garbera Enterprise (www.garberaenterprise.co.uk) were created principally with the needs of the customer in mind. Drawing on a different set of creative skills the sites are informative, visually stimulating, and easy to navigate. And to make sure that they continue to provide the service I expect of them I regularly ask my customers for feedback. This allows for an ever improving customer experience.

# What Can You Do?

## CREATIVITY AND INNOVATION

| Beginner | Phase 1 | Phase 2 | Phase 3 | Phase 4 | Expert |
|---|---|---|---|---|---|
| I like using my imagination | I understand that there are different ways of being creative | I like to think of ways of improving things | I can use problems to generate new ideas | I can evaluate my ideas | I can use previous learning to improve my ideas |

**(Developed by RotherhamReady as partners of HullReady)**

# Six of Thirteen

> **Positive Attitude:** When Henry Ford said: "If you think you can, or you think you can't, you're probably right", he succinctly summed up the influence attitude can have on outcome. Negativity says 'I can't...' It anticipates difficulties and creates images of failure and embarrassment that hold people back. Positivity says 'I can...' It manifests itself in self- belief, constructive thinking, finding solutions and optimism. Many successful people credit their energy, motivation, creativity and success to maintaining a positive attitude. Some say it is the single most important factor, the factor that stopped them giving up, and gave the power to keep going until they achieved their goal.　　　　　**HullReady**

THE lyrics of a song called 'Start all over again' seem extraordinarily apt here. Taken from 'Swing Time', a 1936 black and white musical starring Fred Astaire' it neatly encapsulates the whole idea of not giving up, no matter what life throws at you.

I first heard it whilst doing a bit of late night channel hopping. I'm not particularly keen on musicals but I thought I would give it a go before moving on. Not impressed, my hand began its short journey to the remote control. However, just at the point of pressing the button this song unexpectedly burst on to the screen. I'm not quite sure how it fitted in with the story line of the film because when the song finished I moved on and found some football, but it certainly struck a chord and has stayed with me ever since. Well, not the whole song exactly, but three lines of a chorus. In essence the lyrics advocate that whenever life trips you up or deals you a poor hand, you should never just lie back and accept it, but instead pick yourself up, dust yourself down and start all over again.

And that's exactly what I have done whenever I've been disappointed with a particular result or knocked back in some way. I have always been prepared to get up off my knees, get myself together and as the song suggests, start all over again. Having said that, and as far back as I can remember, being able to maintain a positive attitude has never been a problem for me. My glass is permanently half full rather than half empty. And without a word of a lie, when I first took over as MD of KH Smilers it was this single attribute, more than any other, that gave me the impetus to save the company from bankruptcy and oblivion. KH Smilers was not, as far as I was concerned, going to be consigned to the dustbin of history without a real fight. Therefore, any negativity on my part simply wasn't an option!

Indeed, my positive nature kicked in from the moment I took charge. Unfazed by a £250 black hole in the company finances I set about rebuilding the business. Within days the old product had been ditched and a replacement unveiled in its place. A new company structure was introduced making each director's role and associated responsibilities transparent and unambiguous. And by any stretch of the imagination this was real progress. Now, we could really start to build in earnest!

In what seemed the blink of an eye, resources were identified, market research completed, finances organised, training in hand, a production line established, a marketing strategy agreed and a sales campaign launched. Phew! These were hectic times to say the least, but, on the other hand, hugely satisfying. Seeing each piece of the jigsaw falling neatly and seamlessly into place gave me and the others a massive boost as we prepared to enter the YE Company Programme competition for real.

Furthermore, putting together the KH Smilers 'package' for competition was all about 'I can.....' or in our case 'We can.....' Nobody doubted that this would be a difficult task from the moment we entered the programme. After all, when our YE journey started we were all in Year 10 (14 year olds) from a comprehensive school, whilst virtually all our rivals, locally and nationally, would be Sixth Formers from the state or private sector. Now if that's not a mountain to climb I don't know what is!

But there is nothing like competition to start the adrenalin pumping round the body. It simply added to the optimism and enthusiasm we already felt. Admittedly, our start in the autumn of 2003 can only be described as a disaster. But by early 2004 KH Smilers was back in the competition as serious contenders and there was only one aim: to reach the Grand Final at the Savoy Hotel in London. In my own mind I knew this was our destiny.

Totally without any business background or YE experience at school our pedigree may have been poor but our determination to succeed was second to none. Clearing the first hurdle of Adjudication Day was immensely satisfying and, speaking just for myself here, set me on a path that I can only describe as life changing.

Although the competition was never just about winning or the publicity that went with it, once the team got the taste for it we were greedy for more. Much, much more! As the KH Smilers juggernaut picked up speed there was a definite feeling that we were becoming unstoppable. Award after award tumbled in to our possession. Cheering and clapping fed our ever increasing confidence. Winning was fast becoming an adrenalin fuelled habit. From the KC Stadium through to Barton and Sheffield no teams were safe. They were simply left dumbstruck as a bunch of Year 10s from a comprehensive school in Kingston upon Hull swept them aside on their way to the YE Company Programme Grand Final. Against all the odds, out of 3500 teams in the UK who had started the journey, we had reached the last twelve. Even more significantly, KH Smilers was probably the youngest team to ever reach the final in London. That made us the best Year 10 team in the country. Unfortunately, that's just how it stayed. After all the success in previous rounds the 'Smilers' had to return to the north bank of the Humber empty handed. Deflated and dejected, of course, but out for the count, certainly not. Step up positivity!

After a fall it is better to get back on the bike, or the horse or whatever as quickly as possible and put the tumble out of your mind. And that is just what we did. Going limited was our way of getting back in the saddle. The day I became a real director of a real company was little short of exhilarating. And as for watching the company grow from strength to strength as sales have continued to rise, it has been a source of enormous pride and pleasure.

But running a business at sixteen years of age can be an incredibly frustrating experience. For a start being taken seriously by the established business world, especially the High Street banks, was a struggle of mammoth proportions. In particular, opening a business bank account seemed, at one point, a well-nigh impossible task. Bank after bank turned me down. As soon as my age was mentioned the door was swiftly but politely opened, and I was ushered out.

The problem was that without a business bank account the business was unable to take advantage of any of the trade deals and discounts that the company was offered. No matter how I tried this symbiotic relationship could not or would not be broken. Either way, for quite some time, KH Smilers was stuck somewhere between a rock and a hard place. But I did not give up. No, if anything, it made me even more determined to get what I needed. And eventually the breakthrough came. The Business Department of one bank was at least prepared to talk to me, Lloyds TSB. Our business plan was first quickly but professionally scrutinised. This helped to establish the services that we wanted the bank to provide. In fact our requirements were very simple. All we wanted was a cheque book account in to which we could deposit our hard earned money. Finally, individual identities were checked and addresses verified. Only one problem remained. Assuming the bank agreed to open a business account in the name of KH Smilers Ltd, a responsible adult over the age of 18 would have to be found to countersign the agreement. Like it or not, this was a condition that could not be breached. I was left with little choice. For the greater good I reluctantly accepted. As a result by the end of August 2005 the dreaded business account was up and running.

A month later the first bank statement arrived. KH Smilers Ltd could now start applying for the numerous trade cards that were on offer, and so long as the bank statement was with me the company was never turned down. Even at B&Q it was more amusing than difficult. Once again it was our ages, and possibly the company name, that made us such dubious candidates for a trade card. Either way, they were the first commercial organisation to give us a line of credit, swiftly followed by Staples, the stationery company. This was another small but important step in breaking down the scepticism that surrounded a company run by teenagers who were still at school.

And then later in the same year being short listed for the Hull Daily Mail Business Awards in the Start-Up Business of the Year category showed how far the business had come. Although we did not win, the nomination alone proved that we had been accepted by the local business community. Alright, we would have liked to have won, but we weren't downhearted when we didn't.

Similarly, being approached by Jon Los in 2007, a local entrepreneur and Director of Vista, a garden centre on the outskirts of Beverley, gave credence to the fact that, as a bedding plant specialist, we were having a significant impact in the area. In a blaze of publicity, this environmentally aware centre had opened with the express intention of sourcing as many products as possible from the local region. Furthermore, he was very keen for small local businesses to trade from the premises. As there was plenty of glasshouse space already lying dormant on site he wanted to explore the feasibility of KH Smilers relocating to the site. We were just the sort of company he was looking for – local, vibrant and prepared to take a risk. This would be a huge opportunity for the business to expand both its range of products and its market share. Unfortunately, before any concrete plans could be drawn up and presented to his Board of Directors, Vista was sold and the opportunity disappeared. Were we disappointed, yes, but out of the game, not for a minute!. Rather than dwelling on what might have been, I got straight on with what I could control, and that was running KH Smilers Limited.

Achieving thirteen GCSEs, five GCE A-Levels and a place at the University of Liverpool Medical School, all whilst overseeing the running and expansion of KH Smilers, was also a testament to my positive attitude. More importantly, I had shown that it was possible to run a successful company from the age of fifteen and, at the same time, achieve good examination results. This success also strongly supported my belief that careers in academia and business were NOT mutually exclusive. In fact I would maintain that I benefitted enormously from this unlikely partnership. And still do!

From the very beginning I fully accepted that the world did not owe me a living, and that if I wanted to be successful (at any level) I would need to work hard and earn it. Waiting for someone else to hand it to me on a plate was never going to happen. Indeed, this is not a strategy I would recommend anyone to adopt. For me, the secret, if there is one, is quite simple: success comes in cans, but failure in can't.

## What Can You Do?

| POSITIVE ATTITUDE | | | | | |
|---|---|---|---|---|---|
| **Beginner** | **Phase 1** | **Phase 2** | **Phase 3** | **Phase 4** | **Expert** |
| I understand what a positive attitude is - 'Can do' | I understand that my attitude can affect how I perform | I can keep trying even when things are hard | I am excited by challenges and the opportunities they provide | I don't focus on negative things unnecessarily – I can 'move on' | I use a positive attitude to get the best out of every situation |

(Developed by RotherhamReady as partners of HullReady)

# Seven of Thirteen

**Initiative:** Initiative can be seen as the willingness to take the first step, or make the first move. If no-one was willing to take the initiative nothing would progress. How many people talk wistfully of big ideas they've had, but never acted upon? Sometimes the gap between idea and reality is the hardest one to bridge because it requires tangible action. Taking the initiative includes elements of risk, positive attitude and good judgement. Importantly though, it includes the willingness to 'go for it' – which is essential in a fast paced competitive world where every job, business idea and opportunity will have many people chasing it.

**HullReady**

THE original product choice for KH Smilers – a range of novelty items including Whacky Test Tubes and Crazy Sand – ultimately proved to be a disaster. With no significant sales, a huge debt was soon built up and the confidence with which the team started soon collapsed. The company needed new direction and a new product. As the new MD of KH Smilers I took the initiative to provide both. Deep down I knew I had to 'go for it', and by suggesting that we go into the business of growing, selling and also delivering a range of summer bedding plants the focus and scope of the company changed dramatically. Together with a bold marketing strategy, I strongly believed that KH Smilers could now rid itself of its previous debt, make a healthy profit and as a result make progress in the YE Company Programme.

As it happened all three goals were eventually achieved and, as all things do, passed in to history, but what did not pass in to history was my willingness to keep on developing, to keep on progressing the business. Incidentally, a desire that remains strong even to this day. Maybe this 'go for it' attitude is just part of my nature. If I talk about wanting to do something I will, unless it's absolutely impossible, do it. In fact, the number of times I've heard my dad utter those immortal words, "You're what?" (immediately followed by the silent shaking of the head), doesn't bear thinking about. For example, at 17 organising a week-long trip to Berlin for myself and two friends; going to New Zealand for six weeks work experience as part of my medical degree and finally, never having been a serious runner, or any sort of runner come to that, I have completed not one but two Liverpool half marathons, and, more recently I have applied to run in the London Marathon. Mind you, my application to join this event on two occasions so far, have not been accepted, but I won't give up. Apparently if you are knocked back five times they are obliged to let you run on the sixth.

Throughout the Young Enterprise phase I was constantly using my initiative to make the team more professional and, as a result more successful in the Company Programme. Initially it began with finding someone who could help us to increase our knowledge of plants and how to grow them. This was essential if we were going to convince experienced gardeners to buy our products. Next, organise training that would improve our ability to understand and, therefore, manage our company finances. As you can imagine confidence in this area had been especially low. Organising to have the company presentation videoed whenever possible thus allowing for a valuable means of feedback for developing and honing our skills in this area. And seeking the advice of the local business community on how the team could improve its business practice and networking skills.

All well and good but we couldn't stay as a Young Enterprise company forever. Therefore, on 31 July 2004, as per the rules, KH Smilers, was officially terminated; consigned to the dusty pages of history and destined to never see the light of day again. Or so everyone thought. But they could not have been more wrong.

Throughout August I researched our options on the Internet and sought the professional advice of local business men and women. I was determined that in one form or another KH Smilers would continue trading. Admittedly running a 'proper' business and studying at the same time was never going to be a simple task, but I was resolved in my own mind to show that it could be done. After all, it's not as if we would be starting completely from scratch.

I finally took the plunge the following month, October 2004. The appropriate forms and support materials were quickly down-loaded from the Companies House website and without too much hesitation I set about studying the documentation. Eventually, with care and a lot of patience, everything was filled in correctly. Then, together with the appropriate fee the whole lot was sent off to Wales.

Just three weeks later I received a large brown envelope through the post. Inside was a certificate from Companies House in Cardiff. As from 29 October 2004 we were Company No. 5273331. KH Smilers had been re-born as KH Smilers Ltd. We were now a proper company with proper directors, and officially part of the local business community. The transition from school project to a proper limited company was complete. And for me, losing at the Savoy was no more than an irrelevant distant memory.

Expanding and improving the business was now uppermost in

my mind. Let's face it, the easy option would have been to simply stand still and carry on as we had done the previous year, but that was miles away from the vision I had for the future of KH Smilers. It began by increasing our ability to grow more plants. Initially by investing in a 20 foot Polytunnel and then by adding two further large greenhouses. Capacity increased from 3,000 in 2004 to somewhere in the region of 50,000 plants today. The services offered to the customer have also multiplied. A range of winter bedding plants, two sizes of new hanging baskets, a cheaper refill service of customers' own hanging baskets (including free pick-up), a range of prefilled decorative pots and containers as gifts for special occasions, a refill service of any size containers on site and, as long as the order is local, completely free of any delivery charge. And possibly even more on the way.

Deciding to become a publisher was my second foray in to the world of business. I had just gone back to Liverpool (late August 2008) to start my second year of medical studies when I decided that it was time to record my experiences as MD of  KH Smilers. Part One: 'From the Ashes' was finally sent off to the printers in February 2009. The order was for 1000 books. In the meantime, I had set up Garbera Enterprise Limited to publish and market the book. I'd thought about all the different options that were open to me, but eventually decided that setting up my own company was the best way forward. Although risky all my instincts and business experience were urging me to 'go for it'. And to be honest, it was the only way that the idea of producing a trilogy of books could ever become a reality. If the books were ever to see the light of day it was the only action that I could take to ensure a positive outcome.

In the autumn of 2010 I took delivery of yet another 1000 books, 'Smilers Part Two: Lessons in Enterprise' from the Printer. Happily sales for both books have been brisk, and out of a total stock of

2000 units I have got less than fifty left. Impressive by anyone's standards! Hopefully, the third and final instalment will do just as well.

To go back one year, in April 2009 I entered a competition for the 'Most Enterprising Student' run by the Guild of Students for the students of Liverpool University. Although everyone was telling me that it would probably be won by someone from the Management School rather than the School of Medicine, the possibility of winning £100, no matter how slim, would clearly make the application worthwhile. As the old saying goes, 'nothing ventured, nothing gained'. The doubters were even more vociferous when the short list was announced – myself and, as expected, two students from the Management School! But how wrong they were! Just a couple of weeks later they were well and truly silenced as I returned home with my winner's certificate and, of course, prize money to the value of £100.

Working with Sage UK proved to be another great initiative, first in 2008 as part of a national campaign to promote the Sage 50 Accounts Professional Online program (software that I had been using to run KH Smilers remotely from Liverpool), and then again in 2010 when a film crew turned up to make a short video about my experience of being a young entrepreneur and winner of the 'Entrepreneur of the Year Award 2010'. Freely available to view on You Tube it is especially popular in the UK, and wait for it, Namibia and Swaziland. I expected the UK, but the other two countries, who knows? I can only guess that my charm, expertise and rugged good looks are able to transcend all cultural boundaries. Or it could be just a fluke. I'll let you decide.

# What Can You Do?

## INITIATIVE

| Beginner | Phase 1 | Phase 2 | Phase 3 | Phase 4 | Expert |
|---|---|---|---|---|---|
| I understand that not everything will be done for me | I can see when it is good to do something without being told | I understand that using my initiative can sometimes be scary | I don't let fear put me off using my initiative – I can 'go for it' | I can encourage others to use their initiative | I relish the opportunity to take on a challenge and develop new skills |

**(Developed by RotherhamReady as partners of HullReady)**

# Eight of Thirteen

**Organising And Planning**: Planning and organisation is a key factor in the success of projects and activities. This includes being able to manage time and workload, being able to rank priorities and ration scarce resources against competing claims and the ability to take a project from an idea through to final product despite any obstacles that may arise. These skills can best be learned by 'doing', overcoming problems, evaluating experiences, identifying weakness and planning for improvement in the future.

**HullReady**

FROM the moment I joined KH Smilers in the autumn of 2003 to the present day, my life has been a bit of a juggling act. The only difference is that my juggling clubs, instead of being solid and made of wood or plastic are imaginary and labelled homework, company accounts, order forms, coursework, revision, lectures, web shop, marketing, finance, exams, deliveries, stock, sowing seeds, pricking out, planting hanging baskets, presentations, competitions, conferences, leisure time and so on.

Since the age of fourteen running a business and studying at the same time have been my constant companions. At no point have I ever felt that I had to choose between the two, and on only very rare occasions did the demands of one interfere with the needs of the other. For me it was never going to be an 'either/or' choice but a simple commitment to managing both.

In the final two years at Kelvin Hall School it was all about making sure that KH Smilers was in a position to try and win the final of the Young Enterprise Company Programme 2004 at the Savoy Hotel in London; keeping on top of homework, coursework and preparing for examinations in 9 individual GCSE subjects and a GNVQ in IT; and, last but not least, setting up and running KH Smilers Limited.

On transferring to Wyke Sixth Form College in September 2005 the demands were similar but the stakes somewhat higher. This time it was about managing an ever growing and more complex KH Smilers; studying for a GCE AS Level in French, and GCE A Levels in English Language, Physics, Chemistry, Biology and General Studies; and, of course, applying for a University place to study Medicine.

Then leaving Kingston upon Hull to Study Medicine at the University of Liverpool in October 2007 complicated matters further. Now, I had to run a still expanding KH Smilers from 125 miles down the M62; employ my dad to run things day to day; make new friends; start to pick up on at least five years of new knowledge; and incorporate another company (Garbera Enterprise Limited) to publish the first of three books about the life and times of KH Smilers. The first book, 'Smilers Part 1: From the Ashes' has been available since March 2009 and Book 2, 'Smilers Part 2: Lessons in Enterprise' since October 2010; and as you can see I am writing the third one now. And the key to my success, besides hard work which is a given: the ability to organise efficiently and plan effectively!

By prioritising my goals and recording them in some way, I am able to organise the time available to achieve them. For this reason

I have kept a day-to-day diary for many years now. In fact, I probably started this in Year 10 at Kelvin Hall as a means of balancing the needs of KH Smilers with the demands of the school curriculum. As soon as anything needed to be done I wrote it down. Then at the start of each week I made a list that I stuck to (otherwise there is no point in writing the list in the first place), and as soon as each task was completed it was ticked off. This whole process is now so ingrained in me that it has become second nature. Doing something at the last minute, although sometimes necessary, should be avoided at all costs. I honestly believe that without such an effective time management regime I would not be where I am today.

All this makes me sound like a one man band or even, dare I say it, an unsociable workaholic, but nothing could be further from the truth. Throughout the last nine years I have had the support of modern technology, my parents, fellow directors, friends, Young Enterprise, Hull City Council, Enterprise UK, Charles Cracknell, Hull's Youth Enterprise Bank, Vic Golding of GCS Limited and dozens of other colleagues in the world of business. In times of need this support network has never let me down. Moreover, it is exactly this combination of skills and experience that any budding entrepreneurs need to surround themselves with. It can often make the difference between success and failure.

Setting up KH Smilers as part of the YE Company Programme was all about 'learning by doing'. The challenge was indeed quite straightforward – run a business of your choice as if it operated in the real world. Sounds easy if you say it quickly, but in reality, as the original team found out to their cost, the task was far more complex and demanding than they had at first imagined. Fuelled by the excitement of starting a new venture the team rushed headlong in to the task, and as a result proper organisation and planning were, quite literally, left behind in their wake. Unfortunately, by the time some of the directors realised their error, it was too late. The damage had been done and the business imploded. I was determined not to make the same mistake, organisation and planning would be at the heart of the new company. My mantra was simple: 'Fail to prepare is to prepare to fail'.

At the start, our speedy but highly efficient decision making process left us tired but hugely satisfied. We were in no doubt that the foundations for the resurrected KH Smilers had been well and truly laid. All the major decisions had been taken and, as far as I was concerned nothing had been left to chance. There would be no second failure.

Our first organised training session went remarkably well considering that none of us knew one end of a plant from the other; having said that, we were more than willing to give up our time to learn. To run KH Smilers successfully we needed knowledge and practical skills that we did not really have. Knowing all about the plants that the company would be growing and selling was crucial. Talking to customers without this information was unthinkable. It was all part of understanding the market place and showing the adult community that we knew what we were doing.

In the meantime, our plan to target Parents' Evenings had borne fruit. We had received permission to attend two meetings in the following week – one at Kelvin Hall and the other at a local feeder Primary School. These would be further great opportunities to sell redundant stock (Whacky Test Tubes and Crazy Sand), raise extra funds through raffles or similar events and give out order forms. Moreover, Janet Brumby, in her role of YE Development Manager, offered KH Smilers the opportunity to attend *Venturefest 2004* in the historic city of York on Thursday 5 February. Organised by Yorkshire Forward, and held at the world famous racecourse ground, this business forum would allow us to launch the company formally as well as to sell ourselves as a credible business.  Between us we agreed to attend them all.   Organising and planning for each event was now paramount.

A rota of who could attend each occasion was quickly drawn up. Then a list of what needed to be done to make everything run hitch free was discussed, and subsequently implemented.  IT would concentrate on producing a rolling PowerPoint presentation that would give onlookers details of the new KH Smilers whilst Sales and Marketing volunteered to finalise the draft order form.  Moreover, they would make sure that enough forms were printed so that they could be given out at the two Parents' Evenings as well as displayed at *Venturefest*.  The rest of us busied ourselves with designing a professional looking trade stand that could best show off the products we wanted to sell – Whacky Test Tubes and Crazy Sand as well as the terracotta pots that we had so expertly planted. We also brainstormed other ways of attracting people to our stand. This would be especially important on Thursday 5 February.

Within a few days we were setting up for the first of the two Parents' Evenings.  Fortunately it was held at Kelvin Hall.  The familiar surroundings made it a lot easier as this was to be our first outing as the new and revamped KH Smilers.  Our determination to succeed was massive and as a result the team began to organise the stand to a pre-determined plan as soon as the Entrance Hall was clear of pupils going home at the end of the school day. Moreover, Health and Safety had to be a consideration in everything that we did, particularly as it involved the public.

As the first parents began to arrive we sprang in to action. Obviously some were more receptive to our sales pitch than others, but as the evening progressed it was clear that there was a steady stream of money flowing in to the cash box.  Most parents bought a 10p raffle ticket and many could be seen leaving the building with a range of our products.  Equally important, order forms were being taken home as well as some parents having the confidence in our company to fill one in on the spot. The last act of the evening was to draw the raffle. Although many of the parents had gone home each parent who could not stay wrote their name and telephone number on the back of their ticket. That way one of us would be able to make contact with them the next day and arrange delivery. As it happened it was not necessary. The winning number belonged to a teacher who was still in the Main Hall talking to parents.

Forty eight hours later we were once more selling the company and its products, but this time in one of Kelvin's feeder Primary Schools. Naturally, we stuck with same formula that worked so well in our own school. However, with the pupils being younger we expected to shift more of the Whacky Test Tubes and Crazy Sand. Our instincts on all counts proved to be correct and as a result KH Smilers made another healthy profit as well as walking away with a clutch of completed order forms.

Two down and one to go! Thankfully, not much needed to be changed, but this was a distinctly different event to the Parents' Evenings and, therefore, certain elements needed a little more attention. We would be networking with well-established regional companies so everything about us and the business had to be as professional as we could make it. And to make sure nothing was left to chance we decided to seek further advice from a local successful businessman – Vic Golding of Golding Computer Services Limited. The information that he could provide us with would be invaluable in ensuring that *Venturefest* would not be a wasted opportunity.

The night before the event the whole team came together to make sure nothing was forgotten. With a check list to hand every item that we needed, no matter how small, had been listed and then duly ticked off as ready to go. There could be no doubt that KH Smilers had left nothing to chance. As complete novices, we were as confident as we could be that all the bases had been covered. Barring some natural cataclysmic disaster, our preparations ensured success and not failure.

I was equally as diligent, if not more so, when organising and planning my assault on the real world of business. From our already significant customer base KH Smilers had a huge niche market in to which it could expand. There were lots of people out there, who for one reason or another, could not or would not go to a garden centre to choose and collect their plants. The market place was, as far as I knew, devoid of any service quite like ours. KH Smilers held a virtual monopoly, and by keeping our overheads to a minimum we could offer an affordable personal service to each and every one of our customers.

In many ways the basic KH Smilers business model has remained unchanged. Obviously, over the years the model has been 'tweeked' now and again to either update or to improve the services offered but, at its core the idea is simplicity itself. From a predetermined list each customer can have their choice of bedding plants grown to order and then delivered to their door. With quality guaranteed, what could be easier? What could be 'greener'? And as we worked on a strict 'cash on delivery' basis, there was no risk to the customer. All the risk was ours. More importantly I was convinced that, in terms of price, the business could successfully compete against the more established traders, and in the future have the potential for rapid but sustainable growth.

By the time I went back to school in September 2004 as a Year 11 student the dilemma of what should happen to the company next was on the verge of being resolved. Essentially the problem had boiled itself down to three possible courses of action. As there was going to be four of us in the business the choice of becoming a sole trader was simply not appropriate. Forming a partnership was a distinct possibility but it did not offer the protection of limiting our financial liability. In other words each of us, as individuals, would have been legally responsible for any debts incurred by the business. Even though I was convinced that the new company would never get itself in such a position, as fifteen year old novices in the real world of business, it was a risk none of us could afford to take. That only left me with one option. KH Smilers would have to become KH Smilers Limited.

Undeterred by the weight of documentation, I separated the application form from the support material and began completing the details, double checking everything as I went along. We chose to have equal shares in the company. Our investment of £100 each meant that in the face of financial meltdown our total liability would be £400. Then I downloaded and paid for a legal document known as the Memorandum and the Articles of Association. Without this documentation, which sets out all the legal require-ments of becoming a private company limited by shares, there could be no limited company. Once lodged with Companies House, this particular paperwork would guarantee the status of KH Smilers as a 'Private Company Limited by Shares'. Although there are dozens of provisions within the Articles that define in the smallest detail the exact nature of a private limited company, to me it simply meant two things. First, that the directors could not be taken to court for more than £100 worth of individual debt and second, I could not sell shares in the company to the general public. This was a job well done and set me up perfectly for incorporating Garbera Enterprise Limited just 5 years later.

Finally, the ability to review and evaluate is in my opinion, part and parcel of good planning and organising. After each round of the Young Enterprise competition, for instance, we sat down as a team to analyse the experience, and identify both the strengths and weaknesses of our performance. However, it was the weaknesses that we really wanted to iron out. Therefore, mindful that we should not be over critical of each other as individuals, we engaged in a process that was, in the main, honest and positive. And the results speak for themselves. We couldn't stop winning all the way to the London final. Out of a possible 24 awards, over three rounds, we bagged 13 of them!

Similarly, as KH Smilers has grown and developed as a business I have on a yearly basis reviewed and evaluated the company's performance. As a result, realistic goals and targets could be set for the following season. Future planning, which may involve removing poor sellers from the order form, implementing a new pricing structure, finding new suppliers, introducing a new service or setting money aside for capital projects, is fully informed by such a review. Indeed, as I publish the final part of the 'Smilers' trilogy I am evaluating the prospects of Garbera Enterprise continuing life as a local publisher, particularly as a service for young people, possibly still in education, who may not have the time or the resources to self-publish.

# What Can You Do?

## ORGANISING AND PLANNING

| Beginner | Phase 1 | Phase 2 | Phase 3 | Phase 4 | Expert |
|----------|---------|---------|---------|---------|--------|
| I can find out what I've got to do | I understand why a plan is important | I can apply different planning techniques | I can prioritise my work-load to ensure different deadlines are met | I can evaluate and learn from previous experiences | I can create plans that anticipate changing circumstances |

(Developed by RotherhamReady as partners of HullReady)

# Nine of Thirteen

**Decision Making, Problem Solving And Identifying Opportunities**: Make intelligent and timely decisions and you're on the road to success, but a string of poor and ill-considered decisions can leave you struggling to get back on track. Decision making and problem solving are closely linked. For both it is necessary to work out the likely consequences for any course of action, identify and weigh-up pros and cons, evaluate evidence, consider alternatives and choose and implement the best course of action. Identifying opportunities becomes part of this process – it may be that a brilliant opportunity is spotted when a 'problem' is being solved. **HullReady**

GOOD decision making has a lot to do with that most intangible of qualities, confidence. Difficult to find and yet so easily lost. Just listen to any football manager whose team is on a losing run. If you don't hear the word 'confidence' mentioned several times over, I'll eat my hat! In business it's just the same. Having confidence in your own abilities, and especially in your ability to make the right call at important times, is critical. And this is something I very definitely learnt with KH Smilers. Initially, during the YE phase and then, most definitely, when the company became limited.

At the start of my tenure as MD of KH Smilers I was very aware that two areas of concern had to be addressed immediately. With the clock ticking there was little or no time for lengthy debate or argument. The team was already at least a term behind our local, regional and national rivals in the YE Company Programme competition and, therefore, I took it upon myself to propose solutions that would alleviate those concerns straight away.

First, to ensure the company had a stable platform I put forward a new company structure, and second, to make sure that there was a replacement for the previous range of novelty items I suggested a new and, most importantly, viable product to sell. However, at this point I ought to say that neither of my proposals were the result of a whim or flight of fancy. Before presenting my suggestions to the Board for proper consideration I had spent quite some time weighing up the pros and cons of several possible solutions. In the end I was confident that I had made the right choices and that the Board would support me. I was right. Both were approved unanimously.

Within a couple of days KH Smilers held its second Board Meeting. Even though the early days of January 2004 seemed to be disappearing with undue haste there was no panic. No running around like headless chickens. We knew what we had to do and, as a result, we calmly set about doing it.

Finance was first. The figures made grim reading. The company was in debt to the tune of £250 but with assets totalling only £175. Unfortunately, £170 of that was tied up in unsold stock. The remainder, £5, was the only cash we had. Moreover, our creditors were ringing the school virtually every other day demanding to be paid. We needed money and we needed it yesterday!

Our Finance Director had clearly been giving this matter some thought and immediately suggested a two part solution. First, to sell as many 50 pence Young Enterprise shares in the company as possible (friends, family and teachers would be our immediate target groups) and second, to take every opportunity that could be found to market the now redundant stock – even at a loss!

This was obviously a sound strategy and so, without much further deliberation, a vote was taken. It was unanimous. Shares would be sold and venues for selling Whacky Test Tubes/Crazy Sand would be investigated by Sales and Marketing. As a result, we were all convinced that cash – the life blood of any business – would start to flow in to the company coffers almost immediately.

Next, I confirmed that the company would have access to 3 large greenhouses and the appropriate horticultural training. This was particularly important as none of us had what you might call 'greenfingers'. Furthermore, the first session would start on the following Saturday with a trip to B&Q. There were no dissenters even though it didn't sound like the most exciting thing to be doing after a hard week's work at school.

Although we had agreed that KH Smilers would be growing and selling summer bedding plants, as yet we had no idea which varieties we would be targeting. It was time to do some market research. This was a very important task and we had to get it right. A poor decision at this stage could mean few profits and a lot of unsold stock. Sound familiar? It should do, because that is exactly what the previous incarnation of KH Smilers had done. We were determined not to fall in to the same trap, hence, the massive importance of researching the market that our business would be entering.

After a search on the internet for the top selling summer bedding plants a simple questionnaire that we could all give to keen local gardeners was devised. We probably knew at least 50 between us. This we felt was a good sample size and also offered us a reasonable cross section of different gardeners. Each respondent would be asked to rank in order from 1 to 10 which plants, from our list of 12, they would be most willing to buy. Moreover, as the gathering of this information was so crucial to the next phase of the decision making process we resolved to complete the survey as soon as possible. Just 48 hours later the results were in and we were left in no doubt as to the top ten. As a result KH Smilers would be growing and selling the following summer bedding plants: Impatiens (Busy Lizzies), Pansy, Viola, Verbena, Begonia, Trailing Lobelia, Petunia, Geranium, French Marigold and Salvia.

Whilst the rest of us busied ourselves with designing a draft order form, our Operations Director scoured the internet for a company who could supply the plug plants we needed. Although this was a more expensive way of growing our plants than from seeds, it was safer. We needed to be certain that we had a viable product for delivery in May and plug plants offered us that safety net. Within a few minutes he had found a company in Jersey that could supply all the different varieties of plants that we needed. Delivery was free, and as a reward for buying from this grower KH Smilers would receive, free of charge, several hundred Sparaxis bulbs. For obvious reasons this became the eleventh plant on the order form. There was just one small problem. The French Marigolds were significantly more expensive than the other plugs. Therefore, on my advice (I remembered growing this particular plant for a school project at Primary School quite easily), the team decided to grow the Marigolds from seed. All appropriate details were duly noted, especially prices.

Next, we turned our attention to the plant containers. Luckily, in an attempt to save time some preliminary research had already been done. A plant nursery in the Midlands was selling 7cm pressure formed pots with carrying trays (which were specially designed to support the pots through the growing and marketing stages) very cheaply, as well as offering free delivery. It appeared to be a good choice and was approved by the team with little more discussion. Once again details of size (of the carrying tray) and price were noted down.

Now we were in a position to calculate the number of plants that we could grow. The dimensions of the plant container were in front of us, and fortunately, I had brought with me my calculations for the total area of growing space that was available in the three greenhouses. In seconds we had the answer. KH Smilers could comfortably grow just over 3000 plants. This seemed a huge number, but we all accepted that it would make good economic sense to grow to full capacity as this way profits could be maximised.

However, there was one more calculation that had to be made before we could finally fix the selling price of our plants. And once again with the help of our friendly calculator, it was determined that to grow 3000 plants, the company would need to buy about 350 litres of compost. Although prices were then checked on the internet, the compost would be sourced locally when needed.

However, before committing ourselves to a final order form it was agreed that as MD I would run our decisions past a couple of the gardeners that had been involved in our survey. This would give us the extra bit of confidence that we probably needed to order our plants and containers, as well as to design, print and distribute the KH Smilers plant order form. Forty eight hours later I was able to report back that the two local gardeners had been delighted to check over the decisions that we had made. They fully supported our choice of plants and containers but were a little concerned that we intended to grow the same amount of each plant variety. They offered their expert view on this matter. Obviously we accepted their recommendations on plant numbers without hesitation. Asking for advice and then not taking it was out of the question. At last an order form could be designed and produced and we were free to order plants and containers over the internet. There was a huge sigh of collective relief. And indeed nothing had been left to chance.

Once the YE competition had finished, returning as a limited company to become the latest member of the local small business community was a huge step for us. The decision was not taken lightly as we could well have fallen flat on our faces. But we did the research, honestly evaluated our chances of being successful and fully debated all the pros and cons of implementing such an important decision. And in hindsight, it was undoubtedly the right course of action. After all, KH Smilers Limited is still flourishing and growing eight years on.

As a small business, KH Smilers Limited has come through the recent turbulent economic times relatively unscathed. Admittedly, costs and, therefore, our prices, have risen but the customers have stayed loyal. Indeed, with more people spending greater amounts of time at home, especially in the garden, business has increased. This is great news for the company and its profits. However, it also throws up a recurring dilemma for KH Smilers - a further expansion. If the demand for our plants is to be satisfied the company needs more space in which to grow them.

As I have already said, this is not a new phenomenon for us. To meet customer demand, the company has had to increase production annually since 2004 when KH Smilers was still involved in the YE Company Programme, and barely growing 3000 plants in a couple of my dad's greenhouses. In the eight years that have elapsed much has changed.

During the winter months of 2005 when we spent hours on the cold, wet streets mailing order forms and flyers through people's letter boxes we didn't really know what kind of a response we would get. After such a back breaking task, the hope was that we might reach orders totalling 5000 to 6000 plants. We would have been more than happy to simply double the previous year's target. In the event we need not have concerned ourselves. Throughout February, March and April orders for plants and hanging baskets arrived almost daily through the post. Our revamped web site was now a web shop and produced a steady stream of orders. Similarly, orders via the telephone proved to be a popular choice, particularly amongst our more elderly customers, who found it the most convenient way to place an order. It was at this point that I noticed a potentially serious problem beginning to develop.

By this time it was the second or third week in March. Orders were getting very close to outstripping the supply. Including plants for hanging baskets we had budgeted to grow about 8500 plants. We now had orders for just over 7000. As the new kid on the block the last thing we wanted was to disappoint any customers, so we made the bold decision to increase production to 12000. Quadruple the amount grown the previous year. But where would we grow them and at what cost? As a capital outlay, the funds to purchase a new greenhouse simply weren't available. The cheaper option was to buy more staging for the existing green-houses and a couple of free standing four-tier 'Growhouses'. For one season it would have to do. And it did! The decision to invest had been the right one. Stock flew off the shelves and profits increased significantly. The hanging baskets proved to be particu-larly profitable. By replanting our plants in to a hanging basket we added value and markedly increased the profit margin. This was a service worth expanding in the future.

Once the season was well and truly over it was time to plan for summer 2006. The issue of growing space was the most pressing problem and needed to be resolved before the next marketing campaign could begin. Financing expansion is never easy for any business, but for a company run by a sixteen year old with no collateral to speak of, it is well-nigh impossible. Fortunately, the city of Kingston upon Hull had a bank where age was not a handicap to accessing financial help – the John Cracknell Youth Enterprise Bank. It had been specifically set up with the purpose of giving young people in Hull the financial support they might need to make their ideas happen.

After doing a good deal of research on the internet I decided that a poly tunnel would be a far more cost effective purchase than a greenhouse. As a result, KH Smilers Ltd applied for, and received, a £500 grant. Within a short period of time a 10 x 20 foot poly tunnel was bought and subsequently erected which immediately increased the growing capacity by a further 10000 to 12000 plants. We now had the potential to double our production to 24000 plants.

Therefore, towards the middle of January 2006 the 'Smilers' marketing machine was once again revved up and slipped in to gear. Order forms and flyers were re-designed and printed. Delivery in the local area was now free, and a new service of refilling customers' existing hanging baskets, as a cheaper alternative to buying a new basket, was offered. These were delivered to our existing customers first. Then new areas for expansion were identified. Over the next two weekends the team delivered an extra 1000 flyers and order forms. Clearly, cold, hard work in the middle of winter, but then the extra plants we planned to grow would not sell themselves. It was also the most cost effective way of marketing our business and products. Realistically, we were expecting a return of between 10% and 20% as new orders.

By early April the majority of orders were in and we had virtually sold all of our stocks of plants. The marketing campaign had clearly worked. I was also very pleased to see a significant rise in the number of hanging baskets that had been sold. Refills were also very popular. This seriously increased our profitability and was, therefore, very welcome news. Two months later it was all over. Another summer season had come and gone.

Sometime in August of that year the three of us were discussing the coming 2007 season when we realised two things. Firstly we hadn't yet tapped in to the winter market for bedding plants and, secondly, if we wanted to expand production yet again, we would need to buy another greenhouse.

The first decision was easy. Although entering a new market is always a risky venture, the company had the necessary experience, capital and know how to pull it off. Having said that, I was mindful of the fact that we could minimise the risk substantially if we set ourselves a realistic target – 5000 plants, and confined the marketing to our existing customers. In the event, that is exactly what we did. Moreover, we needn't have worried. The entire stock, including some winter hanging baskets, was quickly sold. Profits were happily banked and the decision to carry on in the future was unanimously agreed.

The second decision would involve more finance. KH Smilers needed a substantial loan. A detailed bid for £750 was, therefore, put together and sent to the Youth Enterprise Bank. I made it very clear why we needed the money and how it would be spent. They did not let us down. By the middle of October a cheque for the full amount was received and banked. Three months later it had been spent, and a large brand new greenhouse stood proudly next to its somewhat older companions. Combined with our existing growing capacity this meant that production in 2007 could be increased to about 32000 plants. This encouraged us to do three things. First, to increase the range of bedding plants on offer, second, to revamp the web shop, making it more user friendly, and third, to offer a new service of refilling customers' own large containers or tubs on site. Finally, new areas were targeted for leafleting. A new season had well and truly begun.

Not wishing to repeat myself over and over again 2008 and 2009 followed in a similar vein. I tinkered a little with the plants we offered, some simply sold better than others, but otherwise I left things alone. I am a strong believer in the old saying that 'if it's not broken, don't mend it'. The only major change, in terms of the practical aspects of the business, happened once I left for University in September 2007. My enforced absence meant that I was unable to complete many of the day to day tasks on site. As a result, I began to employ my dad on a more regular basis throughout the year. However, I could still run the business remotely by using the Sage 50 Accounts Professional Online Package.

So where does all this leave KH Smilers as we head in to 2013? Well, in the last financial year the production of summer and winter bedding plants had continued at a massive 50000 plants. We also filled some 300 hanging baskets and containers. This has ensured a welcome stability in both turnover and profits. The company still holds one third of an acre of land, and as soon as economic conditions allow it is possible that a controlled programme of investment could see the company continue to grow and maybe even expand its range of products. Only time, and the pressures of being a full time doctor, will tell.

On the other hand, setting up Garbera Enterprise Limited was a decision that came out of a solution to a particular problem. Let me explain. Once the decision to recount the life and times of KH Smilers in the form of a book had been made, the thorny question of who would publish it soon reared its ugly head. As a full time medical student and a company director I neither had the time nor the inclination to hawk the book around the multitude of commercial publishers. Having said that, there is an advantage to doing this, namely, once accepted, and in return for a share of the profits, the whole process of producing and marketing the book is taken on by the publishing company, as are all the expenses. Therefore, unwilling as I was to do this, there was only one answer – self publish. And then when the idea of producing a trilogy got the backing of Hull Training, I took the plunge and simply went for it. Risky or not I had to take this opportunity. Now with two down and one to go, I feel that my decision to start the company has been fully vindicated.

# What Can You Do?

## PROBLEM SOLVING

| Beginner | Phase 1 | Phase 2 | Phase 3 | Phase 4 | Expert |
|---|---|---|---|---|---|
| I like to solve problems | I can think about different ways to solve problems | I see new opportunities exist in 'problems' | I can evaluate different options and decide which is best | I reflect on previous experiences to inform my approach to problems | I implement previous learning to create new solutions and can think 'outside the box' |

(Developed by RotherhamReady as partners of HullReady)

71

# Ten of Thirteen

> **Leadership**: Good leaders have the ability to motivate and influence, they get things done – by their own hard work and their ability to engage others. Leadership is a quality that seems to include many of the other enterprise capabilities. Good leadership requires communication, a positive attitude, initiative, creativity and the ability and confidence to negotiate and influence. In adult life good leadership can be the difference between failure and success, satisfaction and frustration and profit and loss.
>
> **HullReady**

LEADING KH Smilers for the last eight years or so has been a privilege most of the time and a chore only rarely. From the start, performing this role encouraged me to develop a host of new skills and brought out leadership qualities in me that I simply didn't know I had. After a secret ballot held in January 2004, I was propelled through the ranks and elevated to the position of Managing Director. This was my opportunity to take responsibility for the company, to lead from the front and to motivate and inspire my fellow directors to heights of achievement we could, at that moment in time, only dream of.

So, what actual leadership skills and qualities did I bring to the team? To be honest, probably very few that would be apparent to anyone at the time. I wasn't what anybody would call a natural born leader. For example, I was not the type to push myself forward. I didn't like taking risks. I wasn't keen on being the centre of attraction. I didn't feel particularly confident in situations that were out of my rather limited comfort zone. I certainly wasn't comfortable telling everyone how good I was at everything – even if it were true. I'm sure you get the picture.

But I am an optimist. My glass is always half full rather than half empty. Once I start a job I will always see it through to its conclusion. I am prepared to acquire new knowledge and pick up new skills whenever it is required. I have a good command of the English language – written and spoken. I can organise for the short term and plan for the future. I am a good listener, approachable and honest. 'Fairness' is my middle name. I am tenacious and will never give up on something until it's absolutely clear that I am fighting a lost cause. I can get incredibly frustrated with technology but I will never let it beat me.

This particular personality trait, which stops me from giving up as soon as something appears to be too hard or too complex, has stayed with me ever since. Whenever my abilities to bring something to a satisfactory conclusion let me down and frustration is goading me in to capitulation, this aspect of my character kicks in. It will keep me on task or on track until I get it right, even if I have to return to the problem a hundred times. But don't get me wrong here. I don't see this as a flaw or something to complain about. This quality has served me well both in my business life and my academic studies. On numerous occasions when frustration with a difficult situation could easily have got the better of me, I have been pulled from the brink and saved by this vein of, for want of a better word, stubbornness.

All very interesting, but what does all this information tell you about my experience of leading KH Smilers for the past eight and a bit years? Well, for a start, it gives you a good idea of the raw materials I started out with. Either deeply hidden or vastly under developed or both, the qualities I already possessed to make me a good team leader simply needed a catalyst to kick-start a chain reaction that would draw out each one in turn. For me that catalyst was joining, via KH Smilers, the Young Enterprise Company Programme in November 2003. It may sound dramatic but it really was, for me anyway, a life changing moment. It set me on a path that, in principle, I am still following today.

Once such important qualities were stirred in to action, the next step was to harness their potential and mould them in to a package that would allow me to provide the strong leadership that KH Smilers required. Unfortunately, this process could not be rushed and time was needed to assimilate all these newly acquired skills. Moreover, there is little doubt in my own mind that the process is still underway, constantly refining, developing and, therefore, improving my ability to manage.

Anyway, from the beginning, and clearly nowhere near the finished article, I did my best to lead from the front. Step by careful step I grew in to the leadership role and within a few short weeks many aspects of the job were indeed becoming second nature. Even I could see that my presence as MD was making a difference, a difference that was edging us towards success rather than failure.

And proof, if any were needed, that I was doing a good job came during the regional final of the YE competition at the Cutlers' Hall in Sheffield. The date was 15 June 2004. Pitted against Skipton Girls' High School, Doncaster College and Leeds Grammar School we went through the usual routine of setting up the trade stand, being interviewed by the judges, performing the company presen-tation and then enjoying a formal dinner. The awards followed soon after. In fact, there were to be six given that evening, the first of which was an individual award. This would be presented to the MD with the best all round skills. Based on the Company Report and interviews with the whole team, including MD, it also carried with it a personal cheque for £100. I remember feeling very nervous, because if I won, which I clearly did, it would be my first individual award. The trophy of a small inscribed glass pyramid from the Institute of Directors, still takes pride of place at home.

Although receiving that award at just 15 years of age was a real high point as MD of KH Smilers, there have also been times when difficult or sensitive issues have needed to be faced and then resolved. Fortunately, these have been far and few between. However, one such situation stands out in my mind and goes back to the final phase of the YE competition.

The rules for the YE Company Programme stated that a team wishing to enter the competition had to have a minimum of six members. No problem there. KH Smilers had been able to comply with that rule from September 2003 when there was a team of eighteen. Unfortunately, for several reasons, that was down to the bare minimum by January 2004. Still no problem, the team was perfectly legal. It was only when the rules for the Grand Final were examined in more detail that alarm bells began to ring. One of the rules clearly stated that any team winning through to the London final could only send a team of FIVE. I immediately consulted with Janet Brumby, the local YE Development Manager, who confirmed my worst fears. One of the 'Smilers' would indeed have to be dropped from the squad and would not be able to travel to the Savoy. I was stunned. How could I possibly take that kind of decision and rob one of our own of this fantastic opportunity? Someone who had shared in all the hard work and dreamt of the ultimate prize would have to stay at home. No way. It was grossly unfair and with the unanimous support of the team I resolved it was not going to happen. Somehow, no matter what the cost to the company, financial or otherwise, the six 'Smilers' who had started the journey in January would be the same six 'Smilers' that would finish it in July! And, more importantly, I was able to keep my word.

Besides leading the team through all the rounds of the YE competition I was just as happy to enter competitions as a limited company. I was not afraid to be judged by the real business community. As a result I entered the Hull Daily Mail Business Awards 2005 in the Start-Up Business of the Year category. KH Smilers was chosen as one of the three finalists. Although we didn't win, I was more than proud of our 'Runners Up' certificate. At 16, why wouldn't you be?

My abilities as MD and young entrepreneur were further recognised towards the end of 2006 when a new website designed to help teenagers start their own businesses came on line. In partnership with Yorkshire Forward (unfortunately now defunct) the Young People's Enterprise Forum had launched the Wildfire website. It was aimed at 14 to 18 year olds who could register to create their own business homepages, and access expert advice to develop their business ideas. I was one of a panel of experts who could be consulted. After being guided through online tasks, site members would receive a copy of their business plan to show potential investors. I was particularly pleased to be involved with this project, as I believed that I could not only identify with the potential problems and pitfalls that might arise, but also offer the practical and positive guidance that any young person trying to start up their own business needs.

So, from my eight years of experience, what skills and qualities do I think a good leader needs to have? Obviously any list, including my own is, by its very nature, highly subjective. I have made no attempt to prioritise or rank them and I make no claim that this list is in any way exhaustive. Take from it what you will, or take it with a pinch of salt. The choice is yours.

- Provide strong but fair leadership. Lead by example.
- Encourage individual excellence.
- Foster teamwork and co-operation.
- Engender a competitive but friendly team spirit.
- 'Motivator' needs to become your middle name.
- Recognising and solving potential problems.
- Provide options and/or alternative solutions.
- Good communication in all its forms and at all levels.
- Provide analysis, insight and focus.
- Conflict resolution that is open and fair.
- Show interest in, and understanding of, all aspects of the business.
- Organising for the short term and planning for the medium/long term.
- Manage people and resources.

And, to coin a phrase, that's that! However, don't let such a long list put you off becoming a leader. It is a steep learning curve for anyone taking on such a role. But just remember that you are not doing ALL of these things for ALL of the time. Moreover, some aspects of the role can always be shared with other members of the management team. In fact learning to delegate and trusting someone else to complete or oversee a particular task is probably a key skill that I haven't mentioned yet. Furthermore, such an act can provide an individual with a valuable training opportunity. At busy times it will even help you to keep sane.

# What Can You Do?

| LEADERSHIP | | | | | |
|---|---|---|---|---|---|
| **Beginner** | **Phase 1** | **Phase 2** | **Phase 3** | **Phase 4** | **Expert** |
| I can take a role on in a group | I understand what a leader is | I am willing to take the lead | I can reflect on the strengths of a good leader | I can confidently lead a familiar group | I can confidently lead an unfamiliar group |

**(Developed by RotherhamReady as partners of HullReady)**

# Eleven of Thirteen

**Making Decisions On Issues With An Economic And Ethical Dimension**: No person, enterprise or corporation operates in a vacuum and every action can have a consequence, positive or negative. Issues which affect people's lives, the environment and society should be considered with integrity and thought. Where previously profit ruled, the rise of Corporate Social Responsibility highlights how increasingly business is being asked to consider the 'triple bottom line' of People, Planet, Profit. Groups like Fair Trade, 1% for the Planet, and Oxfam have done a great deal to increase awareness of issues around sustainability, the environment and the exploitation of Third World Workers. Now, not taking responsibility for the impact a business has in these areas can irreparably damage a company's reputation and diminish a brand's popularity.

**HullReady**

AS a small, local company decision making of this sort at KH Smilers was never going to have immediate or massive global ramifications. But in our own small way the company has made decisions that I believe have had a positive impact on several environmental issues. Indeed, the mantra 'think globally, act locally' fits the company's thinking exactly.

For a whole host of reasons making a profit is crucial for any business, large or small. For example, without such profits investment for the future and opportunities for employment would be seriously limited. But I also believe that this drive for profits should not happen at any cost. At KH Smilers I have always been more than willing to implement any measures that help to reduce our impact on the environment.

From the beginning, we have never used any form of chemical spray to control pests such as greenfly and whitefly, but instead we use natural predators to do the job for us – ladybirds. Over the years, I have spent many happy hours collecting these voracious beetles from plants in the garden before putting them to work in the polytunnel and greenhouses. Moreover, they do a much better job than any spray. Aphids can easily avoid the deadly consequences of a chemical attack, but a ladybird is genetically primed to seek and destroy – there is no hiding place. And as for slugs and snails the easy solution would be to scatter pellets in and around the plants, but I prefer a different approach. Under the cover of darkness all you need is three things, a torch, a bucket and someone who doesn't mind picking off these pesky critters. But, and I have to be honest here, it is this final requirement that prohibits my full participation in the nightly 'huntathon'. I am happy to operate the torch and carry the bucket, but I draw the line at actually touching these slimy molluscs. Yuk! Fortunately, my dad is not so squeamish and the job takes just a few minutes each night. Outside the growing areas I try to encourage hedgehogs to do their thing and intercept these rather unpleasant creatures before they have a chance to attack the growing plants. This, of course, is another reason why I would rather not use slug pellets. Once in the food chain such poisons can have consequences beyond their original target. And the beauty of it all, it doesn't cost me or the company a penny. With no clash of interests, both profits and environment are neatly protected.

Another issue that had to be addressed early on was to do with the growing medium itself. There had been, and still is come to that, a hugely controversial debate, both within environmental and horticultural circles, about the use of peat as an ingredient of commercially produced compost. Driven by the needs of an industry for a cheap and so far abundant resource, the environmentalists claim that massive areas of unique habitat are being destroyed every year. With no way of replenishing the peat, the aim is to outlaw the practice altogether. On the other hand, the growers argue that at the moment, all the available peat-free alternatives are inferior and more expensive. For KH Smilers there was only one thing to do – try both. To be honest there was a difference. As a growing medium the peat based compost produced marginally better plants and, importantly for profits, was significantly less expensive. However, in the end the environmental argument proved to be the stronger. The peat could never be replaced and as a result an eco-system that took millions of years to create, vanquished. Furthermore, I strongly believe that the plant buying public would rather pay more for their plants than see a natural habitat disappear for ever. Therefore, as a small plant nursery I am pleased to say that we have been using peat free products for the last seven years, and as more people have opted for these alternatives so the price has also fallen.

When it comes to the actual containers in which our plants are grown the situation is more clear-cut. Unfortunately, the single 7cm pots and 20 cell plant trays are made from plastic. Light and relatively cheap when bought in bulk, I have yet to find a more suitable or sustainable alternative. Mind you, as oil prices have risen, so have the prices of plastic products, including ours. The only good news in this respect is that in recent years I have found a supplier much closer to home. Therefore, the delivery miles are substantially less. Similarly, with the hanging baskets we sell, I scour dozens of suppliers each year trying to find deals that involve some measure of fair trade. Sometimes the search proves fruitful, but on most occasions KH Smilers just doesn't have the bulk buying capacity to take advantage of what is being offered. This is such a shame, as I would like to feel, even if it's only in a very small way, that my business is helping someone, possibly thousands of miles away to make a living. But I won't give up!

I am also very pleased to tell people that all of our plants are naturally grown. In other words, we don't use any form of heating to speed up the growing process. Customers may have to wait a couple of weeks longer to receive their plants but I really believe that as a result they buy a better product. In my humble opinion the plants are stronger and so live and flower for a longer period of time. In the event of severe spring frosts I use candles, a wholly natural product, to keep the killing cold at bay. Cheap, environmentally friendly and leaving more of a carbon fingerprint than a carbon footprint everyone's a winner.

Finally, on two separate occasions both of my companies, first KH Smilers and then Garbera Enterprise, chose to give something back to the local community that has been so generous with its support. At the end of the YE Company Programme a cheque for £1300 was handed over to the Candlelighters, a charity supporting children with leukaemia. The money represented the profits made by KH Smilers and included the shareholders stake/dividend. They all declined the return of their investment. We were delighted that a charity would benefit from the money that we had earned. Similarly, at the official launch of Book 2 in 2010, and in a bid to help the young entrepreneurs of the future, a cheque for £1000 was presented to The John Cracknell Youth Enterprise Bank . Representing some of the profits from book sales, I see this money as an investment in the future of Hull's young people and repays, in a small way, all those people who had the confidence to invest in me.

## What Can You Do?

### MAKING ETHICAL DECISIONS

| Beginner | Phase 1 | Phase 2 | Phase 3 | Phase 4 | Expert |
|---|---|---|---|---|---|
| I know when I am being fair | I know that my choices impact on others | I want to make a difference | I take and create opportunities to make a difference | I can reflect on the ethical dimension of my actions | I make decisions as a responsible citizen |

**(Developed by RotherhamReady as partners of HullReady)**

# Twelve of Thirteen

**Financial Literacy**: How do you manage a budget? How much do things cost? How much do you need to live? What is profit and loss? Developing a real awareness of how the world of money works is vital. Nothing comes for free. You can work hard and improve what you had, but sometimes things go wrong and you have to start again.

**HullReady**

WHEN I took over as MD of KH Smilers the company was already £250 in debt! As I examined my rather dubious inheritance it became obvious that apart from 'spend, spend, spend', no proper consideration had been given to the financial structure of the business. This was a big mistake. As creditors came banging on the door for payment, the coffers were empty. Negligible sales meant little income and, therefore, ultimately, no way of paying for the goods received. Result, financial meltdown and company directors heading for the hills. The planning that could have so easily avoided this scenario had simply been omitted. Not deliberately I am sure, but just through a woeful lack of knowledge and the understanding of basic financial principles.

Sorting out the finances, therefore, became a top priority. The business, like any family or individual, had to start living within its means. But before that could happen, the debt had to be cleared. This meant that somehow we had to get cash flowing in to the company bank account. This would be done by selling as many 50p YE shares in the company as possible, and by seeking every opportunity we could find to sell the novelty items we already had in stock. Moreover, if we could repay the debt in instalments, there would be some cash available to start investing in new stock. Our creditors were immediately consulted. Fortunately, they were more than willing to support this plan. It would take a little longer for them to get their money, but at least they knew that they would be paid. They could also stop hounding us for payment. That in itself was a relief to all concerned, I am sure!

The next step was equally as important to get right. We had to make a net profit if the business was going to prosper. This can be shown by a simple equation:

## Gross Profit – Overheads = Net Profit

Therefore, getting the costs to stack up was imperative. In other words, our pricing policy had to be accurate. A 'guesstimate' was not going to be good enough. At least there was no VAT (Value Added Tax, currently at 20%) to complicate the calculations. In essence, the maths was quite simple. First, work out how much it will cost to provide the product or service. In the case of KH Smilers, this meant that we first had to establish how many plants we could grow and in what size containers. Originally, we chose to sell in trays of 15 plants, but later changed to 20 (better value for customers). This gave us a fixed size. Next by dividing the size of container in to the available growing space the maximum number of plants that can be grown was obtained. The cost of seeds, plug plants and compost was then accurately established. We now had a fixed cost for our product. By comparing this cost with our competitors a fair and realistic profit margin could be added. And, hey presto, the costing puzzle was complete. All the information that we needed to set a price for our plants was in front of us. Moreover, it was now possible to work out the potential net profit. By subtracting all our expenses (including debt repayment) from the total sales of plants (and novelty items) I could quickly see what the business would be left with. It was good news. We were most definitely in the black. For the first time since I took over I felt a real sense of optimism for the future.

With Garbera Enterprise the story was slightly different in that there was no debt and no redundant stock to sell off. This was a real pleasure. However, before setting a price for each book, a similar costing exercise had to be completed. Apart from the peripheral costs such as purchasing ISBN numbers, setting up the company, designing and running a website, marketing, delivery and distribution, the main costs centred round preparing each book for the printer and then the actual printing itself. Consideration had to be given to the use of colour, quality of card used for the cover, size, the number of photographs, the number of books in the print run, as all had implications for the final price. Getting accurate and specific quotations from different companies is, therefore, vital. Once this price had been established a profit margin was added. Hence, on a print run of 1000 books the final price of £8.99 was established. This also gave me some scope for discounts on large orders.

Therefore, at whatever level, understanding the basics of financial planning is essential. Moreover, no business can afford to stand still in this respect. In an ever changing world, skills and knowledge need to be constantly up-dated. This is especially true when it comes to managing the finances and everyday accounts of any business, large or small. Knowing exactly what is coming in and going out of a business can make all the difference between success and failure. So just over a year ago I decided to take my own advice and sharpen up my own accountancy and book-keeping skills.

The process actually started when I was fourteen years old. I was fully aware of the shortcomings and lack of expertise within KH Smilers. No business studies at school and no business background at home to fall back on, we were very much on our own; in dire need of help. Reading a YE manual or taking advice from an advisory teacher was not going to be enough to save the company from the slippery slope towards bankruptcy. In my opinion, only someone who was actively engaged in the business sector could give us what we needed – information and practical skills to avoid making further financial mistakes. Fortunately with the help of Vic Golding of Golding Computer Services, I immediately created a short term business plan. Any start-up business would invariably begin by completing such a plan, particularly if they were seeking financial help. In essence it focuses on the company goals and the steps by which it intends to achieve them. A good plan would chart a clear path to a successful outcome – a profitable company. And this was just what KH Smilers needed. It would help me, as Managing Director, to set our goals and prioritise actions. So, with an agreed plan in place the business was now able to move forward and attempt to become both successful and profitable. A laudable goal for any new company, but making a profit was particularly important as we had already run up debts of £250. Before we could do much else this money would have to be paid back. It was, therefore, very important to keep a close eye on what monies were coming in and going out of the company coffers. Some attempt had been made to keep a manual set of accounts but they were simply not accurate enough. What we needed was a computer program that would crunch all the numbers and then produce reports as and when we needed them.

Easier said than done! All of these programs can be fairly expensive and the company was certainly in no position to buy one. Fortunately, with the generous support of Sage UK and Vic's expertise, a training programme that could help our business to run more efficiently was soon underway. As the training progressed I quickly realised myself that this accountancy package did a lot more than just help with managing our finances. It gave us more time to concentrate on bringing our business ideas to life and, by using the information stored in our accounts, the software could even help us to plan for the future.

On a more practical level the Sage 50 accountancy package gave us the tools to manage profit and loss, sales and purchase entry as well as the ability to keep track of what comes in and what goes out. Keeping records of our basic transaction details and getting them right was crucial. This package made this information as easy to understand as possible, and was undoubtedly far less complicated than working with columns and figures. But never forget the acronym GIGO – Garbage In, Garbage Out. Any computer software is only as good as the information that is entered. Therefore, to make sure that you always receive accurate reports, double check that the data has been correctly imputed.

Several twilight and weekend sessions later the training was over. It was great feeling to be able to check our financial position almost on a daily basis and see the company, slowly but surely, moving out of the red and in to the black. The business bank account was finally a cause for a smile and not a grimace!

As a result of that initial training all of my financial decisions have been much easier to make. Over the years expansion has been steady but limited to what the companies could afford. Loans have never been sought unless I was sure that they could be paid back on time. In other words KH Smilers and Garbera

Enterprise have lived within their means. Not bad in such difficult trading times, but what about the future? Well, all of my forecasts point to more of the same - healthy profits rather than any losses.

And that brings me nicely to my most recent bout of training. Not wishing to standstill in terms of my ability to manage the accounts of both companies, I have achieved two further qualifications, namely, IAB (*International Association of Bookkeepers*) Computerised Accounting for Business QCF Level 2 and Level 3. These qualifications focus on the role of a bookkeeper, but with a particular emphasis on the Sage 50 Accounting program. Level 2 also covered a host of important areas including:

- Health and Safety
- Risk Assessment
- Money Laundering
- Banking Procedures
- Principles of VAT (Value Added Tax)
- Costing
- Data Protection

Level 3, on the other hand, certainly extended my knowledge of bookkeeping and the Sage 50 program. So, now with my skills fully up-to-date in this area I am certainly better prepared for the future, and for a small fee I am entitled to have the letters **MIAB** (Member of the International Association of Bookkeepers) after my name. There was only one negative, unlike eight years ago I had to pay for my training this time around.

In terms of budgeting, my experience as a student may also be of some value here. It wasn't until I left home at 18 to study Medicine at Liverpool University that the reality of independent living really struck home. Apart from everything else I was learning, having to provide for myself on a fixed income was proving to be a steep learning curve, especially once I had moved in to rented accommodation in my second year. Up until then I was accustomed to dealing with the finances of KH Smilers but as far as my daily needs and expenses were concerned, that was very much taken care of by my parents. If I'm honest, I didn't give that part of my life any thought at all. Obviously I knew from an early age that everything I received wasn't free and had to be paid for, but that's as far as it went. Once at University, however, that situation quickly changed. Now it was my turn to take responsibility for making sure that I had enough money to meet my costs of living. For example, utility bills, food, clothes, leisure activities, travel, books, stationery and a myriad of other little things all had to be paid for. Living independently from home wasn't as easy as I had at first imagined, but at least I had my business experience to fall back on. This proved invaluable. And by applying the same principles I have managed to keep my head above water for coming up to six years. Having said that, living in London for a year while studying for a BSc in Imaging Sciences at King's College, also tested my budgeting skills to the full. Admittedly, my salary from KH Smilers and Garbera Enterprise has helped to bridge any gaps, otherwise, like many students I would probably have had to find part time work to cover any shortfall in the student loans. Mind you, I have still to pay those back. Clearly, having the skill to manage a budget is for life, and not just for Christmas!

# What Can You Do?

| FINANCIAL LITERACY | | | | | |
|---|---|---|---|---|---|
| **Beginner** | **Phase 1** | **Phase 2** | **Phase 3** | **Phase 4** | **Expert** |
| I know that things are not free | I understand people have to work to get money | I can find out how much things cost and budget | I can make good decisions about how to manage my pocket money | I know about different personal finance issues | I am confident about my ability to manage my finances and stick to a budget |

**(Developed by RotherhamReady as partners of HullReady)**

**Product And Service Design**: All the goods and services that are available for consumers to buy have been through some kind of design, development and production process. For a production process to run smoothly and successfully a team has to work well and communicate. For a product to be successful it has to be creative, for a service to survive it has to be well planned.

**HullReady**

I cannot over emphasise the importance of this process to any business. From my own experience the time, effort and sometimes money, expended to get the fine details right is always worthwhile. The fact that KH Smilers, and Garbera Enterprise are still growing and thriving in such a harsh economic climate is testament to all the hard work that has been put in to this particular element. And continues to be - standing still is never an alternative!

Over the years KH Smilers has evolved in to a business providing both products and services. The core product is summer and winter bedding plants, and the key service is delivering those plants free of charge at a time to suit the customer. However, over time individual specimen plants have been added to the core product, and new services including first time planted hanging baskets, refilling customers own baskets (which we collect free of charge), filling customers own tubs and containers on site have been offered.

The production process has changed very little since 2004. Plants grown from seeds are sown indoors, usually towards the end of February or the beginning of March. Exact timing depends on the plants being grown and the medium range weather forecast. Plug plants are ordered in early February. As our own seedlings reach the required stage for transplanting, the plug plants tend to arrive. Bedding plants are transferred to trays with enough cells for 20 plants. Individual plants are grown on in 7 cm pots.

The production of hanging baskets is much more of a creative process in that there isn't a specific formula to work to. In the end each hanging basket, or filled container, is different to every other one produced. This makes the process a far more exciting prospect than it otherwise would be. It is also more profitable than selling the plants as an individual product. By combining the plants in a container or hanging basket we are adding value. Similarly, going on site to fill containers and tubs allows for greater profitability, in that any price quoted reflects that all the necessary plants and materials need to be brought to the site. For some this service is far more desirable as it allows the customer far more freedom to choose what they would like to have planted. This type of work can be very challenging as being creative 'on the hoof' is not easy, but I can guarantee it's always a lot of fun.

Delivering the plants in the early years was problematic as everyone in the company was too young to drive. Fortunately, my parents were willing to provide the necessary transport so long as it was outside of their own working hours. This arrangement worked well until I was old enough to learn to drive. Thankfully, not long after my seventeenth birthday I passed my driving test at the first time of asking. Deliveries could then be centred round my availability rather than my parents. This made life easier for us all. Today, out of necessity, most of the deliveries are done by my dad.

Deciding to become my own Publisher was a neat solution to a difficult problem. On the other hand, the magnitude of the role never really hit home until the text of the first book was complete. Apart from the creative elements which would influence how the book would actually look, both inside and out, the list of other jobs that would establish a smooth production process needed a good deal of thought and attention.

First of all, to complete the book I needed someone to write a Forward. Vic of Golding Computer Services, a successful local business agreed to do it without hesitation. Second, I bought 10 ISBN numbers (only sold in 10s) so that the books could be barcoded. For resale purposes through a book retailer this included the price. I decided on £8.99. Third, organise the content of the book ready for printing. Fourth, find a Printer. On recommendation, I chose CPI Antony Rowe Ltd. Only then could issues concerning book dimensions, number of pages, use of colour, quality of paper and type of stitching be agreed. A quotation duly arrived and after careful scrutiny eagerly accepted. An order for 1000 books was placed and a fifty per cent deposit was lodged with the Printers. The process complete, book production could begin. However, before full scale production was engaged a proof was received. This was the last chance I would have to rectify any mistakes. The next time I saw the book it was ready for sale. Book 2 went through exactly the same process and now Book 3.

Subsequently, marketing, publicity and distribution all needed my attention. A book launch to prospective customers was first, quickly followed by a web site which allowed Internet shoppers to buy and then pay through PayPal. Promotional leaflets were sent to possible buyers, some including a free copy. However, those receiving a free copy were not simply picked at random. Each one was carefully identified as a strong candidate for a sale. As far as delivery was concerned, single copies were sent via Royal Mail, larger orders via a courier service and any that were particularly local, personally delivered free of charge.

Now tried and tested on two occasions, the whole process, from start to finish, has stood the test of time. Carefully developed to meet the needs of the company and to guarantee customer satisfaction, this phase of the operation has only needed minor changes to keep it on track.

# What Can You Do?

| PRODUCT AND SERVICE DESIGN | | | | | |
|---|---|---|---|---|---|
| **Beginner** | **Phase 1** | **Phase 2** | **Phase 3** | **Phase 4** | **Expert** |
| I like making things | I can make something new from my own ideas | I can follow a brief to make something | I can see that a good design meets an identified need | I can evaluate designs and use my learning to improve them | I can create innovative products and services that meet a need |

**(Developed by RotherhamReady as partners of HullReady)**

# Significant Others

ACQUIRING and developing the skills to be successful in business is very important for any would be entrepreneur. But it is important to remember that this is very rarely a solo effort. I have always maintained that my limited success in business has never been just about what I have done. It's been a real team effort. I often think of it as a driver who races in Formula 1. Without the support of scores of people, success on the track would be virtually impossible, no matter how good a driver they might be.

Young people in particular need the help and support of family, school/college and business, especially the local business community. Having the expertise of those individuals who have 'done it' and 'got the t-shirt' is a fantastic resource to draw upon.

However, if I am going to be totally honest, it has been the help and encouragement of my parents that laid the foundation on which my success has been built. This not only applies to my success in business but also in my academic studies. From my first table top sale in aid of LEPRA in which I raised £80 to my recent graduation from King's College, London they have always been there to support me. However, they have never been 'pushy' parents. Neither have they attempted to live their lives through me. Advice and guidance, yes, arm twisting or pressure to follow a particular course of action, no. Indeed, this is confirmed in an interview my mum gave to Sarah Cook, founder of Raising CEO Kids in America, in 2011. This was as a result of Sarah contacting me concerning a book that she was writing, The Parents' Guide to Raising CEO Kids.

Along with over 130 other CEO Kids, Dave is one of the young entrepreneurs featured in 'The Parents' Guide to Raising CEO Kids' written by Dr Jerry Cook and Sarah Cook and published in the US.

### Interview with Mom of Award-Winning Young Entrepreneur Dave Garbera by Sarah Cook on October 20, 2011

Sarah: *When did you notice that Dave was interested in making money/being in business?*

**Mrs. Garbera:** Dave has always liked to spend money and at a very early age he decided that he needed more than we gave him in allowance! At the age of 7 he realized it was easy to sell general household items in order to raise cash for a school charity project. Dave then went on to sell the contents of his bedroom, on more than one occasion, at a car boot sale in order to supplement his allowance! From that moment on we realized that having his own business was definitely an option for Dave.

Sarah: *How did you go about introducing him to mentors?*

**Mrs. Garbera:** Dave always enjoyed coming into work with me and from an early age he was confident speaking to my MD and colleagues and was eager to learn from them, especially as he loved computers.

Sarah: *Are you or your husband in business and if so – do you think that has given you an edge in raising a CEO Kid?*

**Mrs. Garbera:** I have been the General Manager of an IT company for 24 years so Dave has been used to a business environment. This was especially useful when he entered the Young Enterprise competition when he was 14.

Sarah: *What did you to do support him along the way?*

**Mrs. Garbera:** We have always supported Dave from an early age by taking him to car boot sales in order to raise cash. In particular, we have supported him over recent years when he chose to have a business career together with University life. We pointed him in the right direction to carry out his own research.

Sarah: *How did you help Dave stay balanced in all the other things he has to do in his life?*

**Mrs. Garbera:** We both encouraged Dave to continue with the things he enjoyed in life. He has always loved to listen to music and enjoys playing the guitar, keyboard and drums. Music has always been the balance in his life and is very important today. Dave's father took him to his first concert in Copenhagen when he was fourteen and camping at music festivals.

Sarah: *What were some of the challenges that you all faced in helping him become the success he is today?*

**Mrs. Garbera:** The biggest challenge was maintaining a balance and we did not push Dave in any way. We always gave him options and he drew his own conclusions. We strove to support Dave rather than push him. Dave needed to keep his options open and his feet on the ground.

Sarah: *Is there anything you would have done differently that you would be willing to share with other parents of CEO Kids?*

**Mrs. Garbera:** No, there's nothing we would have done differently. We have always listened to Dave and balanced our reactions accordingly. We are very proud of him and his achievements.

Sarah: *Would you share your TOP 3 – 5 tips that every parent of a CEO Kid should implement.*

**Mrs. Garbera:**

1. See your child as an individual and not an extension of yourself
2. Listen
3. Offer Advice
4. Do not push
5. Support

# Help Yourself

PUTTING yourself first is ok. Wanting to work alone is also fine. But not for ever! Learn this lesson earlier than I did, and make a positive decision to work as part of a team, even if it's only for a short time. However, if at this stage I am preaching to the converted, that is, you are already a committed team player, fret not and simply push on to the end. After all, my advice is free and maybe even useful.

Don't shy away from the good old role play. Properly supervised and organised they can provide a genuine opportunity to explore, and then reflect on, all the key skills that help the individual to work as part of a team. Join an established society, club or group whose members are already working together for a common purpose, or maybe you could even start something up of your own, if necessary with adult supervision – a business perhaps. Young Enterprise would be an ideal vehicle for this. The number of people does not really matter, but there need to be enough so that you can practise your team building skills. I can't guarantee that it will all be smooth sailing, but believe me when I say that the benefits will far outweigh any short term setbacks. Go on, don't just think about it try it now. And, above all, remember the saying, "there is no 'I' in team".

Clearly, we all need to learn how to cope with, and manage, risk in our everyday lives. Eliminating all risk is neither possible nor desirable. Therefore, being able to identify a potential pitfall and then in some way mitigate or control it benefits us all. But for me, learning the skills to know when the time is right to take a risk, and then being able to bounce back if everything goes pear shaped is paramount. Unfortunately, there is no magic age at which this can suddenly happen. Everyone's different. It's all down to individual development and, of course, patience. Experience can't be rushed.

The easiest way of starting to take a risk is with your own learning. It took me far too long to realise that getting things wrong was not a bad thing or in some way a failure. Instead it could be turned on its head and seen as a positive learning experience. So don't be afraid of making mistakes, and see them for what they really are – opportunities to make progress and increase confidence.

Once again, running a business, real or simulated, can help to develop and sharpen all of the skills needed to make informed decisions and take calculated risks. You won't always get it right, nobody does, but such activities can help you to avoid the reckless type of decision- making that often leads to major problems, in business or come to that, in life generally. Whether the issues turn out to be personal, financial, or organisational, they can, in the end, prove to be a disaster for the individual or the company. Unhappily, the original KH Smilers learned that lesson too late to save themselves and their business. But it wasn't all bad. Their hapless risk became our great opportunity!

From the outset I would like to make it clear that the acquisition and development of these particular skills – negotiating, influencing, persuading - is not about enhancing an individual's selfish desire to get their own way all the time, or about having the power to manipulate the actions and desires of others for personal profit. In fact, I believe it's exactly the opposite. I see them more as a means of resolving difficult situations and so ensuring, as far as is possible, that the path to a successful outcome remains obstacle free. Whatever the goals, the prudent use of these skills can always be employed to achieve them.

The successful deployment of these skills depends on the individual's ability to communicate, to employ the spoken word. Some people find this easier to do than others, but no matter what your level of ability in this field it is always possible to improve.

Practise is paramount. Get in to the habit of really listening to people. Start with a friend or relative. Ask them to tell you a short story, real or imaginary, it doesn't matter. Your job is to listen closely. On completion repeat the story back to them. Not word for word, that's not the point of the exercise, but recounting as many of the important points as you can remember. As you get better, so the stories can get longer. Similarly, you can write short speeches trying to persuade or influence someone to take a particular course of action. Read them out aloud and get some feedback, especially about the words and language that you have used.

Structured role play can give you the opportunity to interact with others. Done properly and encompassing different scenarios, they can provide valuable insights in to the social and emotional aspects of this whole process. On the other hand starting a business, real or simulated, can locate these skills in a real life business context. By providing opportunities to test your abilities in listening, negotiating, influencing and persuading such experiences are invaluable. Equally, it will test your resolve to carry on if decisions don't go your way.

There are no short cuts to good communication skills. Very simply, you need to learn how to sus out your audience and always remember that you can't talk to everyone as if they were your best mates. Your body language and style of communication can, within seconds, either impress the people you are talking to or, in truth, just as quickly turn them off.

In this respect practise can really make perfect. For example, answering the telephone. In business this skill is absolutely essential, and if delivered poorly could have serious implications for the well-being of the company. Starting the conversation with "Yeah, what do you want?" isn't going to win you any friends or product orders. By the same token coming across as friendly, polite and willing to help can make a world of difference.

The prospect of delivering some sort of presentation can produce a certain amount of anxiety and nervousness. But this isn't necessarily a bad thing. Once you have a script that you are happy with and it's 'fit for purpose', rehearse it. Initially on your own but then in front of a small audience whom you trust to give you constructive criticism. Trust is important, as the last thing you need is for someone to make fun of your efforts. Making a video that you can playback to yourself can also help you to visualise how the prospective audience might see and hear you. I often found that the more I rehearsed the more familiar I became with the material. This resulted in a much more confident delivery. And having this confidence boosted my performances no end.

Many people believe that they are NOT creative because they can't draw or play a musical instrument or make things, but for me such a definition is far too narrow. In business for example, creativity is all about ideas and the courage to implement those ideas. It's about having the imagination to think 'outside the box', to come up with new solutions or novel improvements to real problems.

Once again, by starting a real or simulated business you can provide yourself with an ideal training ground. Just like I did with KH Smilers, the 'safe' environment of a YE company allowed me to experiment with all aspects of the creative process. By interacting with others I was able to develop and hone my skills to the point where I felt confident that I could go on and use them in the real world.

Unlike Data, the super android from Star Trek, we are all liable to make mistakes or errors of judgement, but these events in themselves are not as important as how we react to them. Even dear old Sir Alan Sugar has dropped some clangers in his time, for example his brief but very costly association with a London football club. The very public humiliation he received at the hands of the media nearly broke him, he admits that quite freely, but he didn't take the easy option and just disappear in to the woodwork. No, instead he chose to shrug it off, pull himself up by his boot straps and return to the world he knew best, business. Now, as well as being a famous TV business mentor, he is one of the UK's top tycoons and a multi-millionaire to boot!

The lesson for us all is very straightforward. If we want to achieve our goals, oust negativity and embrace positivity. Forget 'I can't…..' and adopt 'I can…..' Get in to the habit of dispelling images of failure and possible embarrassment before they infect your sub-conscience mind as they will most definitely hold you back, and instead concentrate your efforts on bolstering your confidence and self-belief, qualities that in the long term can only help you to move your life or your business forward. For I have no doubt that there is a compelling link between attitude and outcome. It's not easy, but then no skill worth having comes without some element of hard work.

Deciding to try and develop your willingness to have a go at something, no matter how small the initial steps might be, is always going to be a move in the right direction. It's all about acquiring a mind-set that nurtures the desire for action and drives the demand for progress. Taking the initiative is what stops us standing still and becoming complacent. It spurs us on to achieve bigger and better things.

Therefore, get in to the habit of simply 'going for it'. If you fail so what, at least you will have the satisfaction of knowing that you tried. Learn from the experience and move on. Don't let your ideas simply slip away, untried and untested. Of course, if needs be, seek out the help and advice you need. This can certainly bolster your confidence and help to ease any anxieties over the risks you might be taking. But what would be a whole lot worse is to do nothing and, in weeks, months or even years down the line you are left muttering the saddest words of all, "if only.....". Dreams are fine, but turning your dreams in to reality is better. I know. I've done it!

Clearly, organising and planning are skills that every school in the country encourages and fosters. I don't actually remember having a formal 'planner' in primary school, but I most certainly did when I entered secondary education. Like many other school students I can't say that they were always used for the intended purpose but once I realised that I couldn't store and remember everything I had to do in my head, using a school planner and then a full day-to-day diary was essential. No matter how young, get in to the habit of organising your time so that you can strike an equitable balance between work and leisure. Make lists like I do. I find them very helpful with deadlines. But if you don't intend to stick to them, don't bother. That really is a waste of time!

As ever, being involved in a business, real or simulated, can hone these skills to perfection. I started with Young Enterprise, and so can you. Having said that, I know that in Kingston upon Hull, with the support of the local business community, many children in the primary sector are now taking up the challenge of starting and running a business within their schools, for example the 'Make £5 Blossom' campaign.

In life, just as in business, solving a problem, making the right choice or taking the appropriate course of action is not always as clear cut as we would like it to be. Learning to trust your own judgement to make those important decisions comes with practise and experience. Fortunately, both can be gathered from an early age.

The first step must always be to gather every scrap of relevant information. Without it making a truly well-informed decision will be impossible and, in my opinion, substantially increases the risk of making an error. Once gathered, the information should be used to highlight options or suggest courses for action. Each alternative should then be fully explored and evaluated so that likely consequences, advantages and disadvantages, can be quickly identified. And only then, on the balance of probabilities, should the decision be made and implemented. Moreover, such a process might even suggest new opportunities hitherto unimagined.

Although these skills can be applied to any situation that crops up in our daily lives, being involved in some sort of entrepreneurial activity can bring them to life in such a way that your confidence and your ability to make the appropriate call can be genuinely enhanced. Make that decision to get involved today.

It is said that a leader is someone who rises above the crowd and gets things done. Clearly, for some the ability to lead comes quite naturally. Confidence and charisma seem to ooze from every pore. But for the rest of us mere mortals taking the lead doesn't come quite as easily. The skills have first to be learned and then continually practised until confidence builds and allows them to be used. This takes time and is, in my view, better done in small steps rather than large leaps. For me the initial step was agreeing to join KH Smilers as a Sales Director, a role that I believed held no responsibility for making important decisions. I was ok with that. Mind you, it also helped that I knew some of the people involved. Working with complete strangers, particularly at a young age, is far more daunting. Therefore, if you are able to, do something similar. Then as you gain experience allow yourself to take on more and more responsibilities. Don't be backward at coming forward at this stage. Your confidence to start making decisions will depend on it.

Trying to do right by issues such as pollution, Third World poverty and climate change is something that can no longer be left to the few. As individuals, businesses and countries, we all share a responsibility to care for the planet and its inhabitants. Opting out at any level is no longer an choice. Start by looking at your own life and what you can do to make a difference, no matter how small. For example, don't drop litter, if you smoke stop it, walk or cycle whenever you can, and buy 'fair trade' goods whenever possible. Small changes that if put into practice by millions of people can have massive positive global consequences. This equally applies to any business, large or small. Indeed, if you are tempted to start a business of your own, decisions on suppliers and materials, for instance, could have either negative or positive consequences. The choice will be yours. 'Think globally, act locally'.

I think we are all aware that there are very few things in this life that come without a price tag. It is, therefore, very important that we are all able to manage our finances. Being able to budget to live within our means is a skill applicable to every level of society, from the individual managing their pocket money to the government managing the finances of the UK. Learning these skills can start from a very early age. For example, having to save up for a particular item teaches children the value of money and, more importantly, that there are very few people who can buy whatever they want on demand. But for most of us personal finance issues only really come in to sharp focus when we leave home. Having to live on a fixed income suddenly becomes a reality and to avoid debt, personal needs have to be prioritised. I can only say that having run a simulated and then a real business before going to university, taught me everything I needed to know about debt, budgeting and borrowing money. If you can get the opportunity do the same. I can guarantee you won't regret it.

From a very early age most of us like to make things. My parents tell me, that from being a small child I was often more interested in the packaging than the toys inside. Why? Probably, because I could make something that came from my imagination, my own grand design so to speak. I am sure you have all done the same. Later, as I got older, I was quite keen on making models, although following the instructions was never as easy as the manufacturers claimed. Usually, however, with a bit of help the model was eventually finished. There is something quite satisfying in watching a range of plastic pieces transform in to a complete object, for example, in my case the Millennium Falcon. These activities, and ones like them, are a great starting point in thinking about design and the production process. This led me to exploring how things were made and why they looked as they did. Sometimes I would mess about with paper designs to see if I could come up with something better. Whether they actually worked in the real world did not matter, the fact I was thinking about it, did. But as ever, the real learning started when I got involved with running a business. There is no substitute for this kind of 'hands on' experience. In the first instance it doesn't even have to be real, the process will be the same. Start by identifying a need. Then, challenge yourself to develop a product or service to meet that need. It doesn't have to be totally new but it should have elements that make you stand out from the crowd. Put your own spin on it. Your attempt to launch something that is marketable and attractive to potential customers will mean that every aspect of the design and production will have to be evaluated and analysed. Your skills in this area will, as a result, grow and develop. Go on, have a go!

# The Outro

**"To accomplish great things, we must not only act, but also dream, not only plan, but also believe".**

FROM an early age we all have the sort of dreams where we imagine ourselves to be anything from super heroes to globally famous rock stars, from superstars of sport to ground breaking scientists, from great inventors to billionaire captains of industry. The list is endless. There are no boundaries except for the ones we create for ourselves. Alright, I accept that later in life the dreams may become a touch more realistic, but the important thing is we continue to have the dreams.

Unfortunately, for so many people their dreams remain just that, dreams. For whatever the reason that's where it all stops. They never take the next step. Decisions and choices that, with a little courage, they could have so easily made for themselves are left to others; their lives and destinies now shaped by people who don't always have their best interests at heart, and external forces over which they have very little or no control.

But for me, that's where the excitement of so many possible futures begins, with a dream. As young children anything and everything is possible, just as it should be, but as we get older we start to filter out what is clearly impossible, for example, acquiring the powers of a super hero.

However, we must as adults, be very careful that reality does not stifle the young who can take on negative messages far more easily. We switch them off at our peril. Instead, they should be positively encouraged to practise and develop the skills and qualities that in the future will make them enterprising people and possibly successful entrepreneurs. For example, the 'Make £5 Blossom Campaign, delivers a real business experience to many of Kingston upon Hull's primary school children. Supported in the classroom by men and women from the local business community it is a great advert for doing just that. It doesn't destroy their dreams, but instead enhances them. It encourages them to bring their business dreams in to the classroom and discuss them seriously with their peers, teachers and mentors.

Debate liberally sprinkled with expert advice, slowly but surely begins to channel their dreams in to practical business propositions. And, for the first time, many of the children experience and bear witness to, a process that can actually turn their dreams in to a reality. How fantastic is that? More importantly, it is exactly the sort of positive experience that can then be fostered and nurtured throughout the years at school and college, for example by organisations like the Young Enterprise Scheme and events such as Global Entrepreneurship Week. As a result, young people and adults alike will become confident and properly equipped to make sensible and well informed decisions about the future of their working lives, especially when that decision could involve starting and growing their own business.

But, let's not kid ourselves. To be successful in any walk of life you need dedication and commitment. Becoming an entrepreneur, young or otherwise, is no different. In my opinion you must:

- Have a strong desire for achievement

- Like to be in control

- Seek out opportunities and use resources to fulfil plans

- Believe that you already have or can learn the skills to be successful – the Big 13

- Be innovative and willing to take a calculated risk

Looks and sounds easy. But we all know it isn't. As a result, all the hard work and activity needed to become successful comes with a warning. I can't stress enough the importance of rewarding yourself from time to time. If all you do is focus on business you will undoubtedly burn out and I can guarantee that your energy levels and your motivation will drop off significantly. Therefore, make time for yourself. Choose an activity that will help you to relax and recharge the batteries and as a result you will return to your business refreshed, motivated and ready to go. For me its music and football, but it can be anything. You can also treat yourself to gifts, large or small. Again for me it tends to be gadgets or the latest in mobile phone technology. During stressful periods such treats have helped to lift my spirits and affirm that it is all worthwhile. And to finish, one final piece of advice: **"you will get what you want if you just help people get what they want".**

# Appendix 1

## Managing Director Roles and responsibilities:

- Provide positive overall leadership.

- With the aid of others, to identify and produce a mission statement.

- To help formulate and agree the goals of the company.

- To be responsible at all levels for the performance and well-being of the company.

## Marketing Director Roles and responsibilities:

- Conduct market research.

- Identify potential markets and products.

- With the aid of others decide upon quantity and pricing.

- Work with Sales to devise strategies for customer awareness and product delivery.

- Develop ways of promotion/advertising.

- Prepare, oversee and update the overall marketing strategy.

- Agree sales forecasts.

- Record customer satisfaction.

## Operations Director Roles and responsibilities:

- Contribute to product development.

- With the help of others devise a cost effective manufacturing system.

- Seek to maintain quality whilst reducing costs.

- Balance production with demand.

- Contribute to estimating costs.

- Purchase raw materials.

- Keep inventories of materials, work in progress and the finished product.

- Monitor the safety of the working environment.

- Maintain equipment and tools.

## Sales Director Roles and responsibilities:

- Acquire a sound knowledge of customers and competition.

- Contribute to pricing policy.

- Suggest promotional activities to maximise sales.

- Develop and motivate the sales force.

- Take charge of stock delivered from Operations.

- Manage credit and cash collection.

## Finance Director Roles and responsibilities:

- Produce a financial plan which shows how the company will deliver its profits.

- Devise strategies to ensure results are delivered.

- Agree pricing in order to maximise profit margins.

- Record all financial transactions.

- Forecast cash flow and manage all cash and credit controls.

- Make payments.

- Prepare Profit and Loss Statements and Balance Sheets.

- Control banking and cash security.

- Assists with stock valuation.

## ICT Director Roles and responsibilities:

- Determine the ICT facilities available to the company.

- Advise on appropriate software.

- Provision of ICT training as necessary.

- Ensure accessibility of company website.

- Works with marketing to create a company website and promotional materials.

## Human Resources Director Roles and responsibilities:

- The provision of appropriate training to enable the company mission to be achieved.

- Endeavour to create a harmonious working atmosphere.

- Recognise and utilise individual skills.

- Manage a rewards and sanctions policy.

- Keeps personnel records.

- Records attendance and hours worked.

- Monitors safety.

- Ensures that the company complies with employment law.

## Company Secretary Roles and responsibilities:

- Contribute to and maintain an efficient system of communication.

- Complete and keep safe all company documents and records.

- Administer company meetings including drawing up notification and agenda, and recording minutes.

- Enforces company's *Memorandum and Articles of Association*.

# Appendix 2

- The MD to chair all meetings.

- Meetings to be accurately minuted by a member of the Board.

- Meetings to start and finish on time.

- Agenda to be clear and circulated beforehand.

- Be prepared.

- Stick to the agenda.

- Stay on topic.

- Listen to each other.

- Only one person to speak at a time.

- Do not interrupt the speaker.

- Be polite and do not be rude to each other.

# Appendix 3

## ANSWERING THE TELEPHONE

"Good morning (afternoon or evening). KH Smilers. How can I help you?"

If it is an order take the following details:

- Name

- Address

- Telephone number

- Plants required

Repeat the order back to the customer and confirm the total price

"Thank you for the order. I will contact you towards the end of May to arrange a convenient delivery date. Please feel free to contact me if you would like to confirm any details before then.

Bye."

Once the call had been completed the order would immediately be transferred to an order form and filed away. However, just in case a call was a query about the plants we were selling, each of the team had a crib sheet outlining all the important features of each plant variety. This made sure that we were all giving out the same factual information.

Furthermore, I believe that it created an air of confidence. A potential customer may be more inclined to buy from us if they felt that we actually knew what we were talking about.

## CALL TO ARRANGE DELIVERY

"Good morning (afternoon or evening).   My name is.......... from KH Smilers regarding the plants that you ordered. Would it be possible to speak to (name of customer) please?

I am ringing to arrange a convenient time to deliver your order."

(Arrange a convenient time to suit the customer.)

"The total cost of the order is £..... and we accept cash or cheque on delivery.

I look forward to seeing you then.  Please feel free to ring me if you would like to make any changes to your order or delivery time.

Thank you.

Bye."

The agreed date and time of delivery was then transferred to a chart.  Even though most of our deliveries were very local, we did not want to be double- booked.  There is nothing worse than having to inform a customer that you cannot deliver on a promise that you had made earlier.  Also none of us were able to drive, so any arrangements we made had to dovetail with available transport.

# Appendix 4

**DAVE**

Good morning, ladies and gentlemen and welcome to the KH Smilers company presentation. I'm Dave Garbera, Managing Director, and you will be meeting the rest of the team shortly. We are all in Year 10 at Kelvin Hall School in Hull. This presentation aims to give you a potted history of our company, and perhaps most importantly, to show how the team members have grown and developed along the way – just like our plants! Although our school was keen for us to take part in Young Enterprise, it does not offer Business Studies as a GCSE option, so we had a lot to learn. Initially, we bought in a range of mail order novelty gifts but the sales were disastrous. By Christmas 2003 we had a mountain of stock with no sales on the horizon, £250 of unpaid invoices and only two of the original team members remaining.

In January immediate action had to be taken for KH Smilers to survive. An EGM was called which resulted in a new board of directors and a brand new company image. With no time to lose, we discussed ideas for products and finally after a lot of 'trowel and error' we dug up the idea of bedding plants! This was instantly popular among the group and we quickly began to market the project.

**STU**

Our marketing campaign included a range of themed posters, leaflets, flyers and business cards. As the IT director, it was my responsibility to create and maintain a company web site. I incorporated a staff message board which greatly aided communication. We introduced a company logo and catchy slogan - 'Growing a Smile'. Both are used on our trade stand, company newsletters, and all promotional literature. We have also designed a number of PowerPoint presentations to help promote the business.

## MIKE

Determined not to make the same mistake again we took orders in advance of purchasing seeds and plug plants to ascertain the level of demand. At last our business was' blooming', and we agreed to set ourselves some challenging, yet realistic, sales targets. A lot of effort was put into this, and I am delighted to report that our initial target of 3000 spring sowings has now been met.

## KATHRYN

One of KH Smilers most memorable events was Venturefest York 2004. This was our first real opportunity to promote our company outside of the local area. We learned many new skills on the day – including how to work together in an organised way and more importantly - how to network! We have featured in the Hull Daily Mail and the Business section on regular occasions. The team has also been 'adopted' by The Hull Wednesday chapter of Business Network International who invite us on a regular basis to their 7am breakfast meetings.

Following our success in the Humber finals, the Lord Mayor of Hull invited us to a civic reception, where we were honoured to make history by being the first young people to enter the council chambers and take part in a full council meeting.

## MIKE

Over the past few months our Finance director, Richard Myers and other team members have improved their knowledge of bookkeeping by using a Sage accounting program. Recently we have implemented internet banking, which makes checking the bank balance more of a pleasure, now that it is thriving at £1360, ensuring a healthy dividend for our brave shareholders!

## DAVE

As you can see from the screen, all of our plants are grown organically in three greenhouses. Between the team, we check the plants daily but most of the spade work is done at the weekends. (**STU** Which sadly meant no Sunday lie-ins for the team!). Operations Director Benn Jessney is responsible for quality control. This includes checking for any unhealthy plants that might cause disease. To keep our plants healthy, we use organic methods and strictly prohibit the use of pesticides. I am very pleased to tell you, that all our plants are happy in their new homes!

## STU

So – what does the future hold for KH Smilers? We will be diversifying our products with the changing seasons until 31st July when, sadly, our Young Enterprise year draws to an end. Until then, we are planning to create a range of hanging baskets and plant arrangements. We have also recently been asked to supply table decorations for a Gala Dinner at the prestigious KC stadium in Hull.

## DAVE

This year has been an unforgettable experience for us all, and we have enjoyed working together immensely. Not only have we learned how to run a successful business, but we also succeeded in turning our company round when it had hit rock bottom. Valuable skills for our future careers have also been developed. Things like loyalty, respect for other people's opinions, taking a risk and being responsible for the outcome are all prime examples and it is these things that make us very proud to be here today.

Finally, I hope that we have given you a flavour of the fortunes of KH Smilers since its creation in September of 2003 and we will continue to keep on 'Growing a Smile'! On behalf of the entire team I would like to say thank you for watching our presentation. Thank you.